TEACHING AND PREACHING
THE NEW TESTAMENT

Books by Archibald M. Hunter
published by The Westminster Press

TEACHING AND PREACHING THE NEW TESTAMENT
PAUL AND HIS PREDECESSORS
INTERPRETING THE PARABLES
INTRODUCING THE NEW TESTAMENT
INTRODUCING NEW TESTAMENT THEOLOGY
(REVISED AND ENLARGED)
INTERPRETING PAUL'S GOSPEL
A PATTERN FOR LIFE
INTERPRETING THE NEW TESTAMENT (1900-1950)
THE WORK AND WORDS OF JESUS
THE MESSAGE OF THE NEW TESTAMENT

TEACHING AND PREACHING THE NEW TESTAMENT

ARCHIBALD M. HUNTER

The Westminster Press

Philadelphia

Published by the Westminster Press R
Philadelphia 7, Pennsylvania

PRINTED IN GREAT BRITAIN

CONTENTS

PREFACE

Here is another of my participially-titled series of New Testament books. But this one, containing as it does essays, sermons and lectures, is more of a miscellany than its predecessors. Not all of the chapters are quite new. In some cases 'I have fallen back on a previous train of thought', as the minister put it who was loath to admit that he had preached an old sermon. Two indeed of the essays in Part One were originally *Expository Times* articles which later grew into SCM books (*Design for Life* and *Interpreting the Parables*).

The middle part, whose inclusion was suggested by the Editor of the SCM Press, because the volume was to appear in the Preacher's Library series, finds me in the pulpit rather than the study, yet still concerned, I hope, to expound the riches of New Testament truth.

It is Part Three whose inclusion may surprise some. 'What?' they will say, 'Was P. T. Forsyth a New Testament scholar? We had always supposed him to be a Dogmatician.' To this my answer is, 'Yes, Forsyth was a *Neutestamentler*, and an uncommonly prescient and penetrating one—*vide* chapter XXI of this book.' Besides, it is high time when all the theological world is acclaiming the greatness of Forsyth, that somebody from his own *patris*, Aberdeen, should help to swell the chorus!

The four chapters on Forsyth formed the substance of the 'Sir D. Owen Evans Lectures' delivered at the University College of Wales, Aberystwyth, during the session 1962-3; and I should like here to thank the College Senate for the honour they did me by their kind invitation. My thanks are also due to the Editors of *The Expository Times* for permission to reprint three of the essays and seven of the sermons in this book. Essay 4 was originally a paper read to the *Studiorum Novi Testamenti Societas* at their St Andrews meeting in 1961. Later it appeared in *New Testament Studies* whose Editor has also kindly allowed me to reprint it here.

My warm thanks are due to the Rev. Mitchell Hughes, Librarian of Christ's College, who corrected the proofs and made the index.

A. M. HUNTER

King's College, Aberdeen,
July 1962

Part One

NEW TESTAMENT STUDIES

I

THE NEW ENGLISH BIBLE

THE publication of the New English Bible was the most exciting event in religious publishing for a long time, and the sales of the new book have eclipsed even those of a certain novel which shall be nameless.

Now that the critics have had time to pronounce their verdicts, it is possible to see the New English Bible in a clearer light and to pass a fairer judgment on its merits.

On the whole, it has had a very good press. The poet laureate John Masefield spoke for many—'The work, greatly planned, has been manfully done; that which slept has been awakened.'

On the other hand, there have been one or two malicious and ill-informed critics who said things about the new book which were neither just nor true. Perhaps the worst was an American named Dwight Macdonald, who after admitting that he was not a Christian or even religious, went on to dismiss the book as 'the candy floss Bible' and to call C. H. Dodd the 'foreman on the demolition job' (i.e. on the Authorized Version) whose wrecking crew had performed their task with unerring taste and vigour. Robert Graves, the professor of poetry in Oxford, was not much better. After slating the translators for their version of the healing of the leper, he gave them the Graves version of what they should have written:

In one township, a vitiliginous man caught Jesus's eye and threw himself on the ground crying, 'My lord, you could cure me if you wished.'

Vitiliginous indeed! Yet I suppose that in a democratic society where any Tom, Dick or Harry can set himself up as a Biblical critic, such vitiliginous verdicts were to be expected.

Many people with less exalted names have of course written to the papers about the new book, some few for it, many against it (mostly out of a sentimental attachment to the time-hallowed cadences of the Authorized Version). I myself got into trouble for defending the new version of John 3.16—'God loved the world so much that he gave his only Son.' And when I invoked the opinion of the Johannine expert, W. F. Howard, in self-defence, I was accused of using the *argumentum ad verecundiam* (which I take to be browbeating by appeal to authority)! Nevertheless, I do not deplore such newspaper correspondence. There are worse things people could argue about than the Bible. The great matter is to get them discussing the Bible at all in these Biblically illiterate days.

With these few words of preface, let us get down to business.

I

Most of you know already the story behind the making of the New English Bible.

Just as a Scotsman, King James the Sixth and First, was 'the principal mover' in the making of the Authorized Version, so the idea of the New English Bible was conceived in Scotland.

It was in 1946 that George S. Hendry, an Aberdeen graduate, then a Bridge of Allan minister and now a professor in Princeton, persuaded his Presbytery of Stirling and Dunblane to petition the General Assembly to prepare a new translation of the Bible 'in the language of the present day'. His primary concern was to help the Bible speak more plainly, in general evangelism and in work among the young. In a broadcast at that time he said—

> Everyone who has to teach the Bible to young people must have found, as I have, how formidable a barrier the archaic language presents to them. This is a great pity, because it is when we are young that we should learn to understand and love the Bible. This is a matter of urgency and I think the churches should view it so, for it is their duty to publish the Word of God in language which people can understand.

In that broadcast Hendry also made it clear that such a new translation should embody all the new light on the Bible, new textual light, new linguistic knowledge, etc., which our scholars had long been accumulating.

When the General Assembly agreed, events moved quickly. First, all major (non-Roman) churches of Great Britain were invited to 'come in' on the venture; which they did with alacrity. The next step was to appoint a Joint Committee and to enlist the superb skills of the Oxford and Cambridge University Presses. Finally, three panels of translators were chosen, plus a panel of literary advisers to 'vet' their finished work, and a Director appointed for the whole project—Professor C. H. Dodd, the most eminent Biblical scholar in these islands. By 1948 the work had begun, and in the next ten years the New Testament translation panel held no fewer than fifty-seven meetings, each of which lasted on an average three days.

What were their aims?

The Preface to the New English Bible summarizes them thus: 'To produce a faithful rendering of the best available Greek text in the current speech of our time, and a rendering which would harvest the gains of recent Biblical scholarship.'

More explicitly, a threefold task faced the translators: 'First, to determine the Greek text in any given passage where there are variants; second, to decide what precisely the Greek means; and last, to express that meaning in clear and idiomatic modern English.'

What has been the result of these thirteen years' labour?

II

For the *format* of the New English Bible I have heard nothing but praise. Instead of the traditional funereal black we have a comely volume in green and gold. Gaily bound and elegantly printed, the New English Bible has none of the discouraging features of the Authorized Version, no irritating double columns, no arbitrary verse divisions. The text is printed in paragraphs, and poetry (e.g. the hymns in Luke and Paul) as poetry. Finally, the whole effect is illuminated by sub-titles and cross-headings. Thus Paul's magnum opus is headed THE LETTER OF PAUL TO THE ROMANS, and in the body of the letter we find these sub-titles:

1-8   *The Gospel according to Paul*
9-11   *The Purpose of God in History*
12-16   *Christian Behaviour*

In the same way Galatians bears the sub-title 'Faith and Freedom'; James, 'Practical Religion'; and I John, 'Recall to Fundamentals'. All this is clear gain; it makes Bible reading easier, physically and mentally. On this score the New English Bible cannot be faulted.

III

Nor can it be seriously faulted on the score of the Greek text underlying the translation. Everybody knows that, thanks to the discovery of many new and earlier MSS (e.g. the Chester Beatty Papyri and the Bodmer Papyrus) we can now make a far better Greek text than the famous Forty-Seven could in 1611. It has not been revealed what particular modern critical text served as basis for the translators (presumably it was the latest edition of Nestlé). What we are told is that in every textual crux they judged the readings on their merits and chose that which seemed most likely to represent what the author wrote. In any event, it is indisputable that the Greek text underlying the New English Bible is vastly superior to the Textus Receptus of the Authorized Version, and considerably better than that of the Revised Version in 1881.

Few of the reviewers, therefore, have tried to censure our translators here. Robert Graves is the exception. He accuses them of following 'an inferior Western text' in Gal. 4.14, so making Paul's 'weakness' a physical one when it was quite clear, to Mr Graves at least, that Paul was referring to some 'uneradicated moral weakness' in his own character. On this I will only comment that the so-called 'inferior Western reading' is also the reading of Vaticanus and Sinaiticus, the chief witnesses for the Neutral Text.

For the rest, where I have examined the readings preferred by the translators in doubtful passages, I find much to praise.

Let us take three examples.

In Mark 1.41 (the story of the Leper) the choice lies between 'being moved with pity' (*splagchnistheis*) and 'being moved with anger' (*orgistheis*). Up till now all our official versions—even the Revised Standard Version—have chosen the first reading. The second, which is the harder reading, is preferred by all modern commentators on the Gospel. The New English Bible rightly agrees with them—'In warm indignation Jesus stretched out his hand.' So too in Mark 6.3 it reads (with the Authorized Version against modern scholars like Vincent Taylor): 'Is not this the carpenter, the son of Mary?' instead of 'Is not this the son of the carpenter?' as in Matt. 13.55.

Even more interesting is Matt. 27.16 f. Here the Authorized Version, Revised Version and Revised Standard Version all read—'Pilate said to them, Whom will ye that I release unto you? Barabbas, or Jesus who is called the Christ?' But the New English Bible rightly follows the reading of Theta (the Caesarean reading) here—'Which would you like me to release to you Jesus Bar-Abbas, or Jesus called Messiah?' There can be little doubt that the full name of the robber was Jesus Bar-Abbas, and that in many MSS the personal name has been suppressed out of motives of reverence.

Finally, consider John 19.29. Here the official versions—Authorized Version, Revised Version and Revised Standard Version—all tell us that 'they filled a sponge with vinegar and put it upon hyssop, and put it to his mouth'. There is a difficulty here. The hyssop, a small, wall-growing bush with aromatic leaves, is ill-adapted for presenting a wet sponge to the lips of a crucified man. Now in the sixteenth century the old scholar Camerarius, conjecturing that we had here an instance of dittography, surmised that what John wrote was *hussō perithentes* not *hussōpō perithentes*, i.e. 'putting it on a javelin' not 'putting it on a hyssop'. In recent years a MS (476) has turned up with this precise reading; and the makers of the New English Bible, with much courage, have adopted it: 'They soaked a sponge with vinegar, fixed it on a javelin, and held it up to his lips.'

IV

We are now ready to consider the translation itself. But before we come to it, I should like to say a word about the whole *philosophy* of translation which underlies the New English Bible.

What has been attempted is a new kind of translation. Every school-boy knows that there are two kinds of translation. You can call one literal, the other literary. Kelly's *Keys to the Classics* exemplify the first sort, Gilbert Murray's translations of the Greek plays the second. The first is more or less word-for-word: you substitute an English word for each word in the Greek original, leaving the sentence-structure un-altered. But in the other kind of translation you first of all decide exactly what the Greek means and then render it into idioms which are English to the core. Now this second way is much the harder way, for it will mean recasting many sentences—playing 'cat's cradle' with them, as Ronald Knox put it. But, for the general reader, it is much the better way; because, if you bring it off, you will have made evangelist or apostle speak not like a Greek or Hebrew but like an Englishman or a Scot.

Up till now our official versions—the Authorized Version and still more the Revised Version of 1881—have followed the first way. The New English Bible takes the second way and is a literary translation. And this is why famous verses in the New Testament now wear a quite new look. Thus the opening verse of John's Gospel now reads: 'When all things began, the Word already was.' John 3.16 runs: 'God loved the world so much that he gave his only Son, that everyone who has faith may not die but have eternal life.' And the first verse of I John now becomes: 'It was there from the beginning; we have heard it; we have seen it with our own eyes; we looked upon it, and felt it with our own hands; and it is of this we tell. Our theme is the word of life.'

Now from the modern reader's point of view this is unquestionably

the right way. If you translate thus, much of the foreign—the exotic—
flavour of the original disappears, the numerous 'lo's', for example, and
you begin to forget that you are reading a translation at all. The true
ideal of the translator, said Dr Johnson,[1] is to 'exhibit his author's
thoughts in such a dress of diction as the author would have given them,
had his language been English.' This our New English Bible translators
have sought to do, and we must commend them for it.

What then are the particular excellencies of the new version?

First, *improved accuracy.*

When Martin Luther was translating the New Testament, he got his
friend the Court Chaplain (Spalatin) to borrow some royal jewels that
he might see for himself the colours of the precious stones in the book
of Revelation. In much the same way we are told that when Dr Dodd
and his men were translating the story of St Paul's voyage and ship-
wreck in Acts 27, they took counsel of their classical colleagues in order
to make sure that all details of rigging and route, wind and water, were
quite accurate. The result is a chapter stuffed as full of nautical jargon
as a Captain Hornblower story. Here are some specimen verses:

> But before very long a fierce wind, the 'North-easter' as they call it,
> tore down from the landward side. It caught the ship and, as it was
> impossible to keep head to wind, we had to give way and run before
> it. We ran under the lee of a small island called Cauda, and with a
> struggle managed to get the ship's boat under control. When they had
> hoisted it aboard, they made use of tackle and undergirded the ship.
> Then, because they were afraid of running on to the shallows of
> Syrtis, they lowered the mainsail and let her drive. Next day, as we
> were making very heavy weather, they began to lighten the ship; and
> on the third day they jettisoned the ship's gear with their own hands.
> For days on end there was no sign of either sun or stars, a great storm
> was raging, and our last hopes of coming through alive began to fade
> (Acts 27.14-20).

That is one sort of accuracy. But most of the new accuracy in the
New English Bible is due to the fact that the translators knew far more
about Biblical Greek than any of their predecessors did. (Here the
knowledge of the *Koine,* gained from a study of Egyptian papyri, was
specially valuable.)

Let us take an example. When the younger son in the parable set out
for the far country, the Authorized Version says that he 'gathered all
things together', a phrase which suggests, to us, that he crammed all his
belongings into a suit-case. But the Greek verb used here probably has

[1] Baillie, *Dr Johnson and His Circle,* 229.

the special meaning of 'realize', 'turn into money'. Hence the New English Bible's rendering: 'The younger son turned the whole of his share into cash.'

For another example. Most readers of the New English Bible will have noticed that the New English Bible generally alters the Authorized Version's 'tempt' and 'temptation' into 'test' and 'trial'. This is why, in the Lord's Prayer 'Lead us not into temptation' now becomes 'Bring us not to the test'; and why, in Gethsemane, the Lord's command 'Watch and pray that ye enter not into temptation' becomes 'Stay awake and pray that you may be spared the test.'

On the day of its publication a national newspaper roundly condemned the new rendering of the petition in the Lord's prayer on the score that no Christian ought to shrink from testing. Was this condemnation justified?

Not, I think, on linguistic grounds.[1] In the New Testament the primary meaning of the Greek word is undoubtedly 'test' or 'trial' and the meaning 'enticement to evil' is secondary.

Why then was Jesus so anxious that his disciples be spared testing? Because he knew, as the Psalmist before him knew, how hard it is to come victoriously through such testing: 'Enter not into judgment with thy servant, for in thy sight shall no living man be justified' (Ps. 143.2). Having been himself tested in the Wilderness, he knew how sorely such testing would try his disciples, that only by the sheer grace of God could they hope to come successfully through it. Is it not probable that underlying the last two petitions of the Lord's Prayer—

> And do not bring us to the test
> But save us from the evil one

is our Lord's own experience in the Wilderness?

In short, though I cannot see the New English Bible's rendering of the last two petitions of the Lord's Prayer ever becoming popular in public or private devotions, I do not think that the translators can be faulted here for inaccuracy. And I am quite sure that in such a passage as I Cor. 10.13 the new accuracy greatly enriches the meaning.

Now let us take another, and quite different, example of improved accuracy in the new translation.

In Matt. 23 where Jesus denounces the Scribes and Pharisees as 'hypocrites', no less than eight verses begin with 'Woe unto you, scribes

[1] See the excellent article (to which I am indebted) by Marjorie H. Sykes in *The Expository Times* for March 1962, 189.

B

and Pharisees, hypocrites!' Hence it is commonly said that *Jesus cursed the Pharisees.* He did nothing of the sort. A curse implies a wish that evil may befall the person cursed. But Jesus' sayings here are not wishes at all but highly emotional statements of fact. And so the New English Bible here translates (as also in the 'Woes' on the Galilean Cities), 'Alas for you lawyers and Pharisees.' So much for the improved accuracy of the new version.

The next thing I like about the New English Bible is its *clarity.* The meaning of the original writers stands out with a clearness never before so sharply focused for English readers. Phrases which are difficult or ambiguous in the Authorized Version now become as luminous as English can make them.

Take first the Beatitude: 'Blessed are the poor in spirit, for theirs is the kingdom of heaven.' What does 'poor in spirit' signify? Not of course 'poor-spirited'. Nor again 'the spirited poor', as one socialist rendering puts it. It means 'poor in the *religious sense*'—the sense we get so often in the Psalms. It denotes the people who know their own spiritual need—their need of God, like the publican in Christ's parable. And so the New English Bible translates: 'How blest are those who know that they are poor.'

'I am not ashamed of the Gospel,' says St Paul in Rom. 1.16 f., 'for therein is the righteousness of God revealed.' The word 'righteousness' here is rather a cold, austere, statuesque word suggesting to the ordinary reader the inflexible justice of God. This is gravely misleading. Thanks to our Septuagintal scholars (like Dodd and Snaith) we now know that 'righteousness' here is not static but dynamic, that it is in fact a synonym for salvation. Its root meaning is 'vindication'; and 'the righteousness of God' means 'God putting things right' for his people held in the slavery of sin. Hence the New English Bible rightly renders: 'Here (in the Gospel) is revealed God's way of righting wrong.'

Or take Rom. 4.5. Here the Authorized Version speaks of 'him (God) who justifies the ungodly'. All the sheer paradox of grace—God's free love to undeserving men—is in that phrase. But the Authorized Version's wording does not 'bite' on the modern man's mind as the New English Bible does: 'God who acquits the guilty.' A Judge who lets guilty men go free; it is a thing monstrous at law, but the very essence of God's grace in the Gospel; and the New English Bible makes it pellucidly plain. Law-court terms may not be ideal—our Lord himself used personal ones to express the same truth in his greatest parable—but if the idea has to be put in legal terms, how else can you put it?

This clarity, however, is not merely a matter of phrases; it runs through whole documents. Thus the Sermon on the Mount no longer comes to us in 'hieratic prose' out of the swirling mists of antiquity but as a personal challenge, phrased with inescapable clarity:

> Unless you show yourselves far better men than the Pharisees and the doctors of the law, you can never enter the kingdom of Heaven (Matt. 5.20).

> Forgive us the wrong we have done,
> As we have forgiven those who have wronged us (Matt. 6.12).

> Always treat others as you would like them to treat you (Matt. 7.12).

Of all the New Testament writers St Paul is perhaps the hardest to understand. Therefore it is in his Letters that the New English Bible's clarity is most welcome. The Apostle's long and difficult sentences are broken up, and the logical links in his argument made immeasurably plainer. (In Eph. 1.3-14, for example, we have one sentence in the original Greek. The Authorized Version makes three of it. In the New English Bible the single sentence becomes eight sentences.) Here is one specimen of what I mean, the Thanksgiving at the beginning of I Corinthians. If you have the Authorized Version by you, you may judge for yourselves how superior the new version is:

> I am always thanking God for you. I thank him for his grace given to you in Christ Jesus. I thank him for all the enrichment that has come to you in Christ. You possess full knowledge, and you can give full expression to it, because in you the evidence for the truth of Christ has found confirmation. There is indeed no single gift you lack, while you wait expectantly for our Lord Jesus Christ to reveal himself. He will keep you firm to the end, without reproach on the Day of our Lord Jesus. It is God himself who has called you to share in the life of his Son Jesus Christ our Lord; and God keeps faith (I Cor. 1.4-9).

The third quality I like in the New English Bible is its *modernity* (or contemporaneity). Some time ago Dr George MacLeod deplored the Church of Scotland's practice of dressing up its Moderator in eighteenth-century clothes and making him look like the ambassador from Ruritania. I think he had a point. By the same logic, if the Bible is to make its proper impact on us, it should speak the language of 1961, not that of 1611. The New English Bible does just this. Instead of 'Pray have me excused', it says 'Please make my apologies.' Instead of 'Condescend to men of low estate', it says 'Go about with humble folk.' Instead of warning women against 'broided hair', it says 'No elaborate hair-styles.'

Wholly admirable is the way in which the translators have modernized the monies, the times and seasons, and even the tempests of the New Testament. For example: all the Authorized Versions' 'pennies' have been taken out of currency, and rightly, because they were vastly mis-leading. (In New Testament times a 'penny' (*denarius*) was a whole day's wage for a working man.) Now in the New English Bible the Good Samaritan gives the inn-keeper 'two silver pieces' and the value of the perfume poured over Christ is computed as 'thirty pounds'.

So with the talents. According to the Authorized Version, the Un-forgiving Servant in the parable owed his master 10,000 talents. The average Bible reader may know what a Premium Bond is worth, but he has little idea of the real value of a talent or how deeply 'in the red' the servant was. The New English Bible says he was a man whose 'debt ran into millions', and that is about right. By contrast, the fellow-servant whom he refused to forgive 'owed him a few pounds' (literally '100 *denarii*').

Similarly, 'the fourth watch of the night', at which Christ came to the storm-tossed disciples on the Lake, now becomes 'between three and six in the morning'. The 'days of unleavened bread' appear as 'the Passover season'. And the mighty wind that shipwrecked St Paul is no longer 'Euroclydon' but 'the North-easter'.

These are isolated examples of very successful modernizing. If you want to see how up-to-date the New English Bible can be through longer stretches, the parable of the Prodigal Son provides as good an example as any. As it is too long to quote here, I will choose instead the New English Bible's description of Demetrius of Ephesus and his fellow trade-unionists:

> There was a man named Demetrius, a silver-smith who made silver shrines of Diana[1] and provided a great deal of employment for the craftsmen. He called a meeting of these men and the workers in allied trades, and addressed them. 'Men', he said, 'you know that our high standard of living depends on this industry. And you see and hear how this fellow Paul with his propaganda has perverted crowds of people, not only at Ephesus but also in practically the whole of the province of Asia. He is telling them that gods made by human hands are not gods at all . . . (Acts 19.24-26).

[1] The translators should have kept 'Artemis' here. We cannot imagine the Ephesian crowds getting worked up about so essentially an Italian divinity as Diana.

That might almost be the BBC's political correspondent reporting from Ephesus.

One concession to modernity the translators have not made, rightly, in my view. While most of the Authorized Version's 'thou's' and 'ye's' have gone, they have retained the second person singular when God is addressed, so that (for example) the prayer in Gethsemane reads: 'Abba, Father, all things are possible to thee; take this cup away from me. Yet not what I will but what thou wilt.'

Accuracy, clarity, modernity ... Ah but, you may say, what about beauty? How does the new version compare with the old one here?

I think the answer is that no later version—and certainly not one produced in these slipshod, colloquial days—could ever hope to rival the literary splendour of the King James Version. When the famous forty-seven did their work in 1611, all the omens were propitious. They had such an opportunity as comes perhaps only once in a nation's annals. Not only were those wonderful times, but our language was still young, vigorous, malleable, uncorrupted. In short, the makers of the Authorized Version wrought in the greatest literary era of our history, and their performance matched the times.

Let us frankly admit that our times are not conducive to translation in the grand manner of the Authorized Version. Nevertheless, the New English Bible does give us what it set out to give—direct, virile, modern English—the language of a *Times* leader (as somebody has said) with occasional descents into something redolent of the *Daily Mirror*. (E.g. 'This is more than we can stomach', John 6.60; or 'they came down on the rioters at the double', Acts 21.32.) And if its chief strength lies in plain narrative and clear argument, it can on occasion rise to heights of memorable beauty.

Listen, for example, to the new rendering of some lines from the *Magnificat*:

Tell out, my soul, the greatness of the Lord,
rejoice, rejoice, my spirit, in God my Saviour;
so tenderly has he looked upon his servant, humble as she is.
For, from this day forth, all generations will count me blessed,
so wonderfully has he dealt with me, the Lord, the Mighty One
(Luke 1.46-49).

Here are three of the Beatitudes, no less lovely than in the Authorized Version and certainly more meaningful:

How blest are those of a gentle spirit:
they shall have the earth for their possession.

> How blest are those who hunger and thirst to see right prevail;
>   they shall be satisfied.
> How blest are those who show mercy;
>   mercy shall be shown to them (Matt. 5.5-7).

Finally, hear the tremendous paradoxes in which Paul describes the trials and triumphs of an apostle:

> We are the impostors who speak the truth; the unknown men whom all men know; dying, we still live on; disciplined by suffering, we are not done to death; in our sorrows we have always cause for joy; poor ourselves, we bring wealth to many; penniless, we own the world (II Cor. 6.8-10).

To me this seems quite magnificent.

It would not be idle to pretend that the translators have always brought it off so successfully as this. The new rendering of I Corinthians 13 does not seem to be as good as Moffatt's, and in the *exordium* of Hebrews we miss the majesty of the King James Version. But the only fair way to judge the new translation is to consider its *to ti ēn einai*— 'the thing it was to be'. The one relevant question then is not, Does it match the Authorized Version in literary beauty? but, Does it give us an accurate rendering of the New Testament in contemporary English, so that it will be meaningful to many who find the Authorized Version largely meaningless?

Tried by this test, the New English Bible is a triumphant success. There are many today in our own land to whom the Bible is as little known as it would be in a missionary land. To such people, the New English Bible may be, quite literally, a God-send. Mind you, it will not solve, at one blow, the whole great problem of communication with which the Church is faced today. As Gordon Rupp has said, 'We cannot fob off on the new translation that immense job of teaching and explaining which has to be done by the whole Church at every level', from its Divinity professors to its Sunday School teachers. And let us face this too: no amount of modernizing of the New Testament is going to make Paul's argument in Romans or the conception of Christ as High Priest in Hebrews plain sailing for the twentieth-century reader. Nonetheless it is beyond any doubt that the New English Bible by its clarity, its accuracy and its modernity has rendered the Church notable help in its endless task of getting the Gospel across to twentieth-century man.

This is why I hope that ministers are going to introduce it into their Bible classes—and, on occasion, into public worship when that old magic Aladdin's lamp, the Authorized Version, fails to give the light that is needed. I hope also that our day-school teachers will make it the basis of their Religious Instruction. And I hope that the older among us who know and love the Authorized Version 'only this side idolatry' will try to be patient and not prejudge the new book, remembering always that a moving Elizabethan cadence is a sorry substitute for a truth obscured.

Henry Chadwick has called it 'the Bible for the beat generation'. Let us hope that it may prove to be such, and that we shall see a new turning to the Book of Books on the part of the young men and maidens of this land. 'The light shines on in the dark', says the New English Bible in St John's famous Prologue. God grant that, through it, the light of the knowledge of the glory of God in the face of Christ may shine ever more brightly in the hearts of all our fellow-countrymen.

II

THE UNFAMILIAR SAYINGS OF JESUS

No prophet is acceptable in his own country,
Neither does a doctor work cures on his own acquaintances.[1]

I

THE first half of this saying of Jesus, found fifty years ago in the sands of Egypt, you recognize at once; but the other half is unfamiliar, undeniably apt, and possibly genuine. (Cf. Mark 6.5: 'And he could do no mighty work there.') With its combination of new and old, the saying appropriately introduces this lecture on 'The Unfamiliar Sayings of Jesus'. Scholars know them by the curious name of *Agrapha*[2] (literally 'unwritten things'), the term covering all sayings of Jesus not found in the canonical Gospels which have come down to us from other sources.

What are these sources?

The first is the New Testament itself. As we shall see, St Paul quotes one saying of Jesus not found in the Gospels and echoes another. We can recover one more from an old MS of Luke's Gospel. And the apocryphal *Gospel according to the Hebrews*, a lost variant of Matthew extant in only a few fragments, contains two or three more.

The second chief source is represented by early Christian writers. Sayings of Jesus not found in the canonical Gospels were sometimes quoted by early Church Fathers like Justin Martyr, Origen and Clement of Alexandria.

The third source is the sands of Egypt. Everybody has heard of the papyri, those ancient documents written on papyrus which scholars have been disinterring, during the last half-century, from the rubbish heaps of old Egypt where they have suffered sand-burial for two thousand years. Among many thousands of such documents there came to light, between 1897 and 1935, five fragments containing the sayings of Jesus. One of them was a little parchment-book which an Egyptian woman had hung round her child's neck as a charm against evil spirits.

---

[1] This saying appears also in the *Gospel of Thomas* found in 1946 at Nag Hammadi, in Upper Egypt.
[2] The name was first used in 1776 by J. G. Korner.

Finally, the Mohammedans, who regard our Lord as a prophet second only to Mahomet, preserve about fifty sayings of Jesus in their literature. We cannot be sure that any of them is genuine, but two are worth quoting:

As Jesus one day walked with his disciples, they passed the carcass of a dead dog. The apostles said—'How foul is the smell of this dog!' But Jesus said, 'How white are his teeth!'

The other is an inscription found on the wall of a mosque near Delhi.[1] It reads,

Jesus, on whom be peace, has said: This world is a bridge. Pass over it. But do not build your dwelling there.

This world is a bridge, from time to eternity: not the ultimate reality, but only a transition to it. Use it as such, but don't think to make your permanent abode on it. Might not Jesus have said this? Jeremias doubts it. But when you remember that the saying can be traced back to pre-Mohammedan times and note how like its teaching is to our Lord's parable of the Rich Fool, you may well be inclined to disagree.

So let me take up with you the question of the genuineness of these and other sayings ascribed to Jesus. Their total, if we include the Mohammedan sayings, exceeds a hundred. How do we decide whether a saying is genuine or not? In many cases a decision is tolerably easy. The saying in question may flatly contradict what we know of Jesus from the canonical Gospels, i.e., may be completely 'out of character'. If someone credited Sir Winston Churchill with the saying, 'I've been a pacifist all my life', you would be sceptical and rightly so. So it is with many sayings ascribed in extra-scriptural sources to our Lord. For an example: our Gospels, and especially St Luke, are at pains to emphasize the special place our Lord had in his heart for women. When therefore we find some Egyptian Christians who believed in celibacy crediting Christ with the dictum 'I came to destroy the works of the female', we need have no hesitation in pronouncing it false.

Other people wrongly attributed to Jesus something said by a prophet or a psalmist; whilst other sayings are so clearly grotesque that no one in his senses would believe that Jesus said them. Thus, some early Christians make Jesus say: 'My mother, the Holy Spirit, took me and carried me by one of my hairs into the great mountain Tabor.' Need we say more?

Roughly speaking, we have two tests for determining whether a saying be true or false:

[1] On this saying see Jeremias, *Exp. Times*, Oct. 1957.

(a) *External Evidence.* We must be sure that the source which quotes the saying is early and reliable, and of course, if several such early and reliable sources agree, we may be very sure indeed.

(b) *Internal Evidence.* The saying in question must agree in style and content with what we know of the mind of Jesus from our canonical Gospels. If it does not, we do well to be suspicious.

I need not weary you further with technicalities. Enough to say that a succession of scholars from Alfred Resch to Joachim Jeremias have gathered and sifted these sayings with minute and scholarly care. The result is to leave us with twelve to twenty sayings which seem to pass all tests with flying colours, and may be regarded as genuine.[1] It is a small total, but some of the sayings are very vivid and valuable, as I now propose to show.

Let us start with three *stories* about Jesus.

(a) In Codex Bezae, one of the oldest Gospel MSS, at Luke 6.5 a scribe has inserted a story about Jesus after the narrative about the plucking of corn on the Sabbath:

> On the same day seeing a man working on the Sabbath, Jesus said to him—O man, if thou knowest what thou doest, blessed art thou. But if thou knowest not, thou art accursed and a transgressor of the law.

Both in style and content this little story rings true. I need not remind you how strictly in our Lord's day the Scribes and Pharisees kept the Sabbath. On the Sabbath you weren't allowed even to fry an egg or walk more than half a mile. And yet Jesus seemed almost to go out of his way to heal people on the Sabbath. Why? Was it simply a humanitarian concern to insist that man is greater than any institution? This may be partly true, but it fails to explain the words with which Jesus wound up the Cornfields controversy: 'So the Son of man is Lord also of the Sabbath.' There is something deeper here.

Let us recall that the Sabbath enjoined in the Law was regarded as a kind of ritual foretaste of the true Sabbath, i.e. the Messianic Age. The Law Sabbath was the shadow; the Kingdom of God, or Messianic Age, when it came, was to be the reality. (Hebrews makes much of this idea.) If this is the right clue, the reason why the Scribes and Pharisees were so angry at Jesus' apparently cavalier treatment of the Sabbath was that it involved the claim that the Messianic Age had begun and that he himself, as Messiah, was Lord of the Sabbath.

---

[1] Jeremias believes 21 genuine; J. H. Ropes (*Hastings Dictionary of the Bible*, vol. V, 344) thinks 10 trustworthy, and 24 possibly so.

Now come back to our story about the Man working on the Sabbath. Some have thought he was doing agricultural work. More likely, he was engaged on some labour of love. Jesus accosts him: 'If you are doing what you are doing because you know that the time of the law and the prophets is over and the Kingdom is here, you are blessed. But if your working on the Sabbath is sheer impudent defiance, your law-breaking deserves to be condemned.'

It seems to me that the innominate scribe who inserted this little story just where he did showed uncommon insight.

(b) Irishly enough, the next Unfamiliar Story is very familiar. Yet the tale of the Woman taken in Adultery (John 7.53-8.11), though it stands now in the canonical Gospels, belongs to the *Agrapha*. Every student of the New Testament knows that the story is no true part of the Gospel of St John, though most of us are just as sure that if anything in the tradition about Jesus is authentic, this story is. (It may have come from the *Gospel according to the Hebrews*, as Papias apparently said.)

If I dwell on the episode for a moment now, it is because I want to mention the new understanding of it which we owe to the late T. W. Manson.[1]

To understand it, we have to notice, first, that like the Tribute Money story, it is an attempt to trap Jesus, and, second, that in the story itself Jesus ironically plays the role of Roman judge.

Consider the trap set by Scribes and Pharisees. If Jesus sanctions the execution of the woman, he usurps the power of Rome who alone could inflict capital punishment. If he forbids it, he contradicts the law of Moses. Faced with this dilemma, Jesus writes in the dust. Why? In accordance with the practice of Roman criminal law, the presiding judge first wrote down the sentence on a tablet and then read it aloud from the written record. Thus, by his action, Jesus says in effect: 'You are inviting me to usurp the function of the Roman governor. Very well, I will do so, and in the approved Roman fashion.' He stoops and pretends to write down the woman's sentence, after which he reads it out to them: 'Whosoever among you is without sin, let him be the first to cast a stone at her.' Jesus defeats the plotters by going through the form of passing sentence in the Roman manner, and yet so wording the sentence that it cannot be carried out.

The Dominical dialectic in the cause of compassion was surely never more wonderfully displayed.

[1] *ZNW* 44 (1952-3), 255 f. Manson cites evidence for the practice of Roman judges, e.g. *Speratus proconsul decretum ex tabella recitavit* (Acts of the Scillitan Martyrs).

(*c*) Our third story was found in that little book which an Egyptian woman hung round her child's neck as an amulet. It tells how Jesus encountered a chief priest in the Inner Court of the Temple.

Jesus took the disciples into the place of purity itself and walked in the Temple area. A Pharisee named Levi, who was a chief priest, met them and said: 'Who has given you leave to walk in this place of purity and inspect these holy vessels without first bathing yourself and even without your disciples washing their feet? . . .'

At once, the Saviour stopped with his disciples and replied: 'You are here in the Temple? Are you then clean?'

He answered: 'Yes, I am clean. I have bathed myself in the pool of David. I went down into it by the one stair and I came up by the other; and only when I had put on clean white clothes did I come here to look at these holy vessels.'

The Saviour said to him: 'Alas for the blind that see not! You have washed yourself in flowing water in which dogs and swine lie night and day, and scoured your outer skin just as harlots and flute-girls do theirs, anointing and beautifying themselves to arouse men's desire, though inwardly they are full of scorpions and all evil. But my disciples and I, who according to you have not bathed, have bathed ourselves in the living waters from above.'

That is the story, and on many counts it is to be judged authentic.[1] Levi complains that Jesus and his disciples have broken the Temple rules by not washing themselves before entering the Inner Court. We must not suppose that Jesus was being irreverent. The rule that a clean person should take a bath before entering the Inner Court was a rabbinical regulation, without basis in the Law, which Jesus rejected. To Jesus' question, 'Are you clean?' Levi says, 'Yes, I have bathed in David's pool and put on clean clothes.' This, replies Jesus in effect, is no purity at all. The foulest men might lie night and day in such water and be no cleaner than before. Levi has cleansed only his body. Even loose women, says Jesus, do this in pursuit of their business. But he and his disciples have bathed in the water of life. It is the same point as he makes in Mark 7: inward defilement is the only possible defilement in God's sight. The only real purity is that of those whose hearts have been washed clean by the grace of God.

II

Now let us turn to something different. Four of our genuine *Agrapha* concern discipleship. One of them is preserved by Tertullian who tells us it was spoken on the way to Gethsemane:

[1] Jeremias, *The Unknown Sayings of Jesus*, 36-49, to which I am much indebted in this paper.

No man can gain the kingdom of heaven who has not passed through temptation.

We are reminded of the words ascribed to the Lord in the Epistle of Barnabas (7.11): 'Those who will see me and attain to my kingdom, must lay hold of me through pain and suffering.'

More striking is another saying on the cost of discipleship. We recall how often in the canonical Gospels Jesus was wont to warn off all who light-heartedly proposed to follow him, bidding them count well the cost. So it is in this Unfamiliar Saying preserved by Origen:

He that is near me is near the fire,
And he that is far from me is far from the kingdom.

Someone had offered to follow Christ. Have you considered what you you doing? he asks. To be near me is to be near fire (cf. Luke 12.49)—the fire of tribulation and suffering. In other words, it is dangerous to be with Jesus—you may end up on a gibbet or a martyr's pyre. Would you then turn back, as the Rich Young Ruler did? Ah then, says Jesus, you would be missing the Kingdom of God. The fire is only a way—a way through to the glory of God.

Yet, though Jesus can be stern with such light-hearted candidates, he can also cheer his men with words full of hope and confidence, as in the Saying, found at Oxyrhynchus, which begins familiarly:

For he who is not against you is for you

and goes on *un*familiarly:

He that stands far off today will tomorrow be with you.

The saying shows our Lord's unbounded faith in God's power to turn foes into friends. It is a Dominical *Nil Desperandum*. The opponents of today may be the disciples of tomorrow. Not many years later it was to find remarkable fulfilment when Christ's most intransigent foe became his most intrepid apostle.

The last Unfamiliar Saying addressed to disciples is quoted so frequently in early Christian writings that its genuineness is beyond dispute:

Show yourselves tried (*dokimoi*) moneychangers.

or, in its fuller form preserved by Clement of Alexandria:

Show yourselves tried money-changers,
rejecting much, but retaining the good (*to de kalon katechontes*)

a saying clearly echoed by St Paul in I Thess. 5.21 f.:

> Test (*dokimazete*) all things:
> Retain the good (*to kalon katechete*)
> And abstain from all bad coinage (*eidous*).

As always, Jesus goes to real life for his illustration. When one of the money-changers who did business in Jerusalem at Passover time, was not sure of a coin offered him by a pilgrim, he would let it fall on the glass-covered table and the sound it made would tell him whether it was good or bad money. This is the background of our Saying in which Jesus was doubtless warning his disciples against false teachers who might easily delude them. 'Don't be deceived,' he says, 'learn from the money-changers, and acquire a sharp ear for all that is false.' The Saying has not lost its relevance. There are still men who debase the coinage of Christ's realm and peddle counterfeit gospels among the unwary. We have a Christian duty to test and try their pretensions and, where necessary, expose them for the shams they are.

III

Two Unfamiliar Sayings concern the Providence of God and our prayer to him. The first, found at Oxyrhynchus, says quite simply:

> He himself will give you your raiment.

This is reminiscent of the great passage in the Sermon on the Mount (Matt. 6.25-34) where Jesus depicts Lord Raven[1] who neither sows nor reaps and Lady Anemone who neither spins nor weaves, but whom God feeds; and he concludes: 'Shall he not much more clothe you, O ye of little faith?'

Our Saying is of the same tenor. Jesus, we may suppose, is sending his disciples out on a mission. He forbids them to carry money. But will they not starve and have nothing to clothe themselves with? 'O you little-faiths,' says Jesus, 'haven't you a Heavenly Father? Can't you trust him? He himself will provide your raiment.'

The other Saying, which deals with prayer, is preserved by Clement of Alexandria, and by Origen whose version is fuller:

> Ask for the big things
> And the little shall be added unto you:
> Ask for the heavenly things
> And the earthly shall be added unto you.

---

[1] Jeremias, *The Parables of Jesus*, 49.

When you pray, says Jesus, put first things first: God's Kingdom, not your own concerns. If you do this, you may rely on him to remember your needs. The perfect example is of course the Lord's Prayer where we are bidden first to pray for the hallowing of God's name, the coming of his Reign, and the doing of his will, and only when we have done this, are we encouraged to ask for provision (our daily bread), for pardon (Forgive us our debts) and for protection (Deliver us from evil).

IV

Every student of the Gospels knows that Jesus gave his disciples a Design for Living, of which the Sermon on the Mount provides a summary. In this Design the most distinctive thing is the Law of Love, or *Agapē*, which, as you know, Jesus made the master-key of morals. One of the most beautiful expressions of it is to be found in a Saying which, according to Jerome, occurred in the lost *Gospel according to the Hebrews*:

Never be joyful
Except when you look upon your brother with love.

'Brother' here means fellow-countryman, not fellow-disciple. So long as a follower of Christ cherishes hateful thoughts about somebody he knows, he has no right to be glad. A true disciple is only happy when every barrier of bad feeling between himself and the other man is down.

Alongside this Saying we may set the other one which St Paul quoted to the Ephesian elders at Miletus (Acts 20.35):

Remember the words of the Lord Jesus, how he said, 'It is more blessed to give than to receive.'

If the Greek word for *than* has an exclusive force here, as it has in Luke 18.14, the true translation may well be: 'Giving is blessed, not receiving.' In any case, for the friends of Jesus the rule of life must be the conquest of selfishness. And is this not another way of saying *Agapē*?

Two more Sayings—one about Judgment, the other about work— may bring our little *florilegium* to a close. The first we owe to Justin Martyr. 'Wherefore also,' he writes, 'our Lord Jesus Christ said:

In whatsoever things I find you, in these will I also judge you.'

Our Lord is looking away to the great Day. When he comes in glory, he will not go peering into the past; he will take men and judge them, as he finds them. And blessed are those whom he will find abounding in the work of the Lord.

The other saying, which was found at Oxyrhynchus and reads like a saying of the exalted Christ, deals with work and worship. If the Iona Community has a favourite *Agraphon*, this must be it:

> Wherever there are two, they are not without God:
> And where there is one only, I say I am with him.
> Raise the stone, and thou wilt find me:
> Cleave the wood, and there am I.

Notice the two kinds of work mentioned. Lifting stones and splitting wood may sound like the dreariest kind of labour, and the least spiritual. No, says Jesus, even such labour may be transfigured by a hidden glory. As in Matt. 18.20 he promises his presence to the two or three who gather in his name, so here he assures it to the humble toiler who believes in him. What seems like cheerless drudgery may be lustred by the presence of the Saviour.

On that note let me close. The Unfamiliar Sayings are not many, which I take to be proof that the Evangelists did their work so well that only stray bits here and there were left for later gleaners. Yet, few as they are, they are always interesting and vivid, and not seldom memorable and challenging. They do but underline the impression which the canonical Gospels make on any candid reader: 'Never man spoke like this.' With Peter we say, 'Lord, to whom then shall we go? Thou hast the words of eternal life.'

III

THE MEANING OF
THE SERMON ON THE MOUNT

THERE are few forms of literature more ephemeral than sermons. Of one sermon only can it truly be said:

> Age cannot wither it, nor custom stale
> Its infinite variety.

After nineteen centuries the Sermon on the Mount still haunts men. They may praise it, as Mahatma Gandhi did; or, like Nietzsche, they may curse it. They cannot ignore it. Its words are still powerful to rebuke and to inspire. Like some mighty magnetic mountain, it continues to attract to itself the greatest spirits of our race, so that if a vote were taken there is little doubt men would account it the most searching utterance ever made on the moral life.

Yet if men admire it, they do not agree about it. Some think it all 'plain sailing'; others think it impossible. Some judge it to be the heart of Christ's message to men; and others call it 'a sentence of doom' or 'the greatest indictment of sin in human history'. Some talk as if its precepts were meant for all men; others describe it as 'an ordination charge for the Twelve'. What is the truth about the Sermon? And what is its relevance for us today who live in other times, under other skies, and are vexed by other problems? Let us take a glance at some answers to these questions which have been given in this twentieth century.

I

Let us start with the question, What is the relation of the Sermon on the Mount to the Gospel?

The late Mr Gandhi once said: 'The message of Jesus is contained in the Sermon on the Mount, unadulterated and taken as a whole.'[1] Many people in our day have been of the same opinion. It is one of the popular heresies of our times—a heresy much propagated by the popular

[1] C. F. Andrews, *Mahatma Gandhi's Ideas*, 93.

c

press when it writes on religious topics—that the Sermon is the sum of the Gospel, all else being the mystification of the professional theologian.

No reputable New Testament scholar any longer believes this; but the heresy lives on in many minds and needs to be refuted. One way of doing this is to ask, What did the earliest Christians mean by the Gospel? It was certainly not the Sermon. 'To the Apostles,' said Sir William Robertson Nicoll, 'the insistence on the Sermon on the Mount as the sum of Christianity would have appeared a relapse into a hopeless paganism.' This, however trenchantly stated, is a true judgment. When St Paul reminded the Corinthian Christians of the fundamentals of the Gospel he did not summarize them thus: 'Blessed are the poor in spirit etc. Ye are the salt of the earth. Resist not evil. Love your enemies. Be not anxious for the morrow. Do to others as you would have them do to you.'

What he wrote was:

I delivered unto you, as fundamental, what I also received, that Christ died for our sins according to the scriptures; and that he was buried; and that he hath been raised on the third day according to the scriptures; and that he appeared to Cephas; then to the Twelve . . .' (I Cor. 15.3 ff.).

In short, the earliest gospel was not good advice, but Good News. It told of a Divine act rather than of a Divine demand. It is what we have learned in our day to call the *Kerygma*. For the earliest Christians the central thing was not the Sermon on the Mount but the Cross on the Hill and the Empty Tomb, and the power and glory of God made manifest therein.

The other way to settle the matter is to read the Sermon on the Mount itself and consider gravely just what it involves. If some people did this thoughtfully, they would be less ready to cry out, 'Give us less theology and more Sermon on the Mount.' Let any man seriously consider what is implied, say, in Christ's exposition of the 'higher righteousness' (Matt. 5.21-48), and then let him ask himself what good news—what gospel—is to be found there. If God means that, in order to be saved, we must completely fulfil all these demands, then we are all doomed to be damned.

No, the Sermon on the Mount is not the Gospel. How it is related to it, we have yet to consider. Let it be sufficient meantime to say that if the heart of the earliest gospel is the coming of the Reign of God in Jesus Christ incarnate, crucified and risen, the Sermon preserves for us Christ's own design for life in that Kingdom.

II

The Sermon, then, being part of Jesus' 'good advice' rather than of his 'good news', the question arises, What kind of moral manifesto is it?

Prima facie, the Sermon seems so simple and straightforward that a man might be pardoned for supposing that there would not be much difference of opinion about its interpretation. Yet scholars in this century have held almost as many views of it as of the Preacher himself. Let us look at only four of them now.

We may start with Tolstoy who exemplifies the literal and legalistic approach to the Sermon. It is well known how in his latter days the great Russian novelist turned social reformer and found the blue-print for his new society in the Sermon. For him, it was the new law of Jesus abrogating the old law of Moses, and its kernel was to be found in Matt. 5.21-48, with its commandments to be literally obeyed. 'Swear not at all,' said Jesus. This means (argued Tolstoy) an end to all oaths, even in law-courts. 'Resist not evil,' said Jesus. This means: scrap the police force and other resisters of evil. (It can also mean: let thugs and gangsters have their own sweet way. But Tolstoy did not worry about this.) In fine, the Sermon was the new moral law for Christians, to be strictly and literally fulfilled. Let men only do this, and we should have the Kingdom of God on earth.

How differently the Kingdom appeared to Albert Schweitzer of Alsace! For him it was completely eschatological, to be understood only in terms of pre-Christian Messianism and apocalyptic. So far from being any sort of man-made Paradise on earth, it meant the catastrophic irruption of God into history, bringing with it the Day of Judgment and an abrupt end to this world as we know it. The imminence of this Kingdom was the burden of Jesus' preaching.

What then are we to make of the ethic of Jesus in general and of the Sermon in particular? Schweitzer's answer is famous: 'an ethic for an interim.' Just as in war-time exceptional laws are promulgated to cover the time of emergency, so Jesus' ethic was an emergency ethic for his disciples' use during the brief interval between his preaching and the cataclysmic coming of the Kingdom of God. Since, however, the world did not come to an end in AD 30, the ethic of Jesus can have little obvious relevance for Christians in the twentieth century. (Schweitzer's own career since then is a glorious refutation of what seems the logic of his theory.)

Neither Tolstoy nor Schweitzer made many converts to their views.

A much more popular approach to the Sermon in this century has been to regard it as a *Gesinnungsethik*—'an ethic of attitude'. Herrmann and Dibelius took this view. Jesus (they said) was not laying down laws at all. He was indicating attitudes and suggesting the essential inward disposition which ought to characterize his disciples. Spiritual freedom, not any new legalism, was his concern, and he knew that the development of moral personality comes with such freedom. Therefore his ethical teaching, often expressed in the form of sharp paradox, deals with what we should be rather than with what we should do. The danger in this view is that we may be tempted to water down our Lord's teaching; but it has at least this merit (which Schweitzer's had not) that it makes Christ's teaching usable by the modern disciple.

The fourth and last view we will notice may be called the dogmatic approach. It recognizes the rigour of Christ's teaching in the Sermon, and proposes a theological way out. A notable German expositor of this view was the late Gerhard Kittel, first editor of the famous *Wörterbuch*. English readers will find a similar approach in Dr A. R. Vidler's *Christ's Strange Work*. 'The Sermon on the Mount,' says Vidler,[1]

> is not the essence of Christianity; it is the fulfilment of the Law rather than of the gospel. Since it discloses what is implied in the Old Law, it is a terrifying summons to repentance, and the culminating part of Christ's strange work. As we listen to His words that shall never pass away, we find ourselves under the spell of a kind of righteousness to which we cannot even begin to attain.

Thus, the purpose of the Sermon is to bring home to us the awful fact that we are sinners, and so prepare us for Christ's proper work, which is the forgiveness of sins made possible by his atoning death.

What is the Sermon on the Mount? A new law? An ethic for the interim? A *Gesinnungsethik*? Or a terrifying summons to repentance? None of these answers is devoid of its element of truth. St Matthew, at any rate, would like us to think of it as a new law. Since we live 'between the times', in a sense the ethic of the Sermon is an ethic for those who live between the coming of the Kingdom and its final consummation. Because the Sermon gives us 'direction, rather than directions', and is deeply concerned with being rather than doing, we may say that it is an ethic of attitude and disposition. And it is a plain fact of experience that the Sermon, by its revelation of the pure will of God, does reveal to us our sinfulness and our desperate need of Divine forgiveness.

[1] Op. cit., 63.

III

This short survey of twentieth-century interpretations of the Sermon has prepared the way for the constructive part of this study. We propose to put forward four theses concerning the ethic of the Sermon.

(1) *It is a religious ethic.*

(2) *It is a disciples' ethic.*

(3) *It is a prophetic ethic, not a new law.*

(4) *It is an unattainable ethic which, as Christians, we must yet try to attain.*

(1) It is a religious ethic. Few will dispute this. Biblical ethics always presuppose Biblical religion, or rather they grow out of it, are its practical expression in life and conduct. This is true of the Decalogue. It is no less true of the Sermon. Its postulate is faith in God—faith in the Father whom he revealed—as its sanctions—rewards and punishments, the imitation of God, etc.—are religious sanctions. But we must go further than this. Jesus' ethic implies the whole gospel of the Reign of God which was the central theme of his preaching. And Jesus declared that that Reign had now arrived—had begun with himself and in his ministry.

So we have to do with both a Divine indicative and a Divine imperative. But the imperative is founded on the indicative. The indicative may be expressed like this: 'God has manifested his saving Rule in Christ.' The imperative will then run something like this: 'Therefore let all who accept the Rule of God live in a new way—the Kingdom way.' What the new way should be, the Sermon tells us.

(2) It is a disciples' ethic. This is really a corollary of the previous conclusion. The Sermon is fundamentally disciple-teaching. It is addressed to those who are to be the nucleus of the new Israel.

Even if St Matthew had not told us that the disciples formed the audience for the Sermon, there is enough in it to lead us to the same conclusion. The Beatitudes are clearly addressed to 'committed' men. The Lord's Prayer is a Disciples' Prayer. 'Lord, teach us to pray, as John also taught his disciples.' The sayings about salt and light point in the same direction. And many other sayings in the Sermon, including the final Parable of the Two Houses, are obviously spoken to men prepared at any rate to make the venture of discipleship.

The point need not be laboured, for our experts are agreed about it. 'Spoken not to the world but to the Church,' says Gore.[1] 'Given to the

---

[1] *The Sermon on the Mount,* 15.

new Israel,' comments T. W. Manson.[1] 'Ripe teaching for ripe disciples,' declares Montefiore.[2]

(3) 'The Sermon on the Mount,' said B. W. Bacon, 'is not legislative but prophetic. It does not enact, but interprets. It does not lay down rules, but opens up principles.'[3] James Denney said the same thing in a letter to Sir William Robertson Nicoll: 'It would be a great point gained if people would only consider that it was a Sermon and was preached, not an Act which was passed.'[4]

All down the Christian centuries, from St Matthew's day to Tolstoy's, some men have tried to find in the Sermon a new law. The proof that it is *not* such is in the Sermon itself, as A. D. Lindsay has shown:

> Human laws are based on calculations of how most men may reasonably be expected to behave. It is assumed that with a reasonable amount of effort such rules will get themselves kept. A law that is not going to be kept, which asks of people more than they are most of them at all intending to give, is a bad law. It would be of no use making a law or moral code in order to put pressure on men and women to be saints. That the Sermon on the Mount does ask us to be exactly this, in itself shows that it cannot both be regarded seriously and yet treated as legislation. For Jesus told men not as a command but as a revelation and a hope that men are to be perfect even as our Father in heaven is perfect.[5]

In other words, the ethic of the Sermon does not begin to square with what we understand by law.

We reach the same conclusion if we consider Jesus' conflicts with the Scribes and Pharisees and the religion of legalism generally; for at bottom it is a conflict between the prophetic spirit, which deals with persons and principles, and the legalist approach, which always wishes to frame a code of morals telling people how they must act in any particular case. But we need not elaborate the argument here, for it has been admirably expounded by Professor T. W. Manson in his *Teaching of Jesus* (p. 300 f.). Christ does not traffic, as the legalist does, in rules and regulations to cover every conceivable act of conduct. He lays down deep and far-ranging principles. He enunciates the aims and ideals which ought to govern the lives of men who are living in that new order of grace which Jesus calls the Kingdom of God.

(4) 'All this Sermon on the Mount business,' says one of Rose

[1] *The Teaching of Jesus*, 294.
[2] *The Synoptic Gospels*, vol. II, 27.
[3] *The Sermon on the Mount*, 109.
[4] *Letters to William Robertson Nicoll*, 71.
[5] *The Moral Teaching of Jesus*, 96 f.

Macaulay's characters, 'is most saddening. Because it's about impossibilities. You can receive a sacrament, and you can find salvation, but you can't live the Sermon on the Mount.'

This dictum poses the final question, 'Can we use the Sermon on the Mount today, and if so, how?'

Most of us would agree that, as Christians, we cannot dodge the issue, either by saying with the man of the world, 'You can't live the Sermon on the Mount, because it's about impossibilities,' or with the Roman Catholic Church, 'This teaching is not for the rank and file of Christians but for a certain few specially called to lead the religious life.' Christ in the Sermon does set before us a real design for living which challenges every earnest Christian. He does tell us (1) the kind of people we ought to be; (2) the influence we ought to exert in the world; (3) the kind of way in which we ought to behave socially; (4) the kind of worship we ought to give God; (5) the attitude we ought to have towards earthly and heavenly treasures; and (6) the way in which we ought to treat our fellow-men.

'Relevant in this sense,' a man may admit, 'but is the Sermon practicable?'

Here, it seems to me, we must avoid two extreme ways of answering the question. First, we must reject the view which holds that the purpose of the Sermon is simply to 'knock us down'—to show us how utterly we come short of the pure will of God. Jesus meant the Sermon to be a good deal more than a mere counsel of God's perfection; or what is the point of the Parable of the Two Houses? On the other hand, those who hold that Jesus meant his precepts in the Sermon to be practised and that men do in fact live according to the pattern shown them in the Sermon, seem to be refuted by the argument from experience. When Hans Windisch argued for the 'fulfillability' of the Sermon, Rudolf Bultmann replied with an *ad hominem* question, 'Will Windisch claim that he fulfils the demands of the Sermon on the Mount? Or does he assume that some other man does? Then why not?'[1]

Yet Jesus meant his ethic to be more than a blue-print for Utopia. Further, we must never forget that the Sermon is an ethic for those who call Christ Lord and Saviour, for those who have entered the Kingdom of God and are promised the power and help of the Holy Spirit. In other words, we are not asked to scale the heights of the Sermon in our own unaided strength.

In that assurance we can face the challenge of its demands. And

[1] *Glauben und Verstehen*, 199.

beyond question the Sermon does give us stimulus and guidance for the adventure of Christian living. Its standards ought to be before us when we make personal decisions of Christian action. In any given moral dilemma, the Christian may ask himself, 'What light and leading may I derive from the principles and precepts of my Lord, as I know them from the Sermon?' And having done this, he will be the better able to deal with specific moral choices.

The Sermon, then, is our standard and ideal. Of course, it will always be beyond us. That is as it should be—

> . . . a man's reach should exceed his grasp,
> Or what's a heaven for?

Yet if none of us ever reaches the heights to which Christ summons us, this is but an illustration of the tension between the ideal and the actual which must ever mark the life of Christ's disciples in this world. For we have to live our lives at once as citizens of this world, with all its trials and temptations, and as citizens of the Kingdom of God.

Our conclusion is that of Professor William Manson. 'Christ's ethic stands for the unattainable which we are yet bound to attain.'[1] Though we, no more than the first disciples, can never hope to reach the ideal in this fallen world, we are summoned day by day, with the help of the Holy Spirit, to make the effort.

[1] *Jesus the Messiah*, 85.

IV

CRITICS' CRUX
Matthew 11.25-30

THESE are perhaps the most important verses in the Synoptic Gospels. Discussing them in 1927, the late Claude Montefiore[1] candidly confessed that as a Jew he would like to prove them spurious, because, if it could be shown that Jesus had really uttered them, orthodox Christianity would have received notable encouragement. This, however, he thought very unlikely, and he went on to predict that, as the years went by, the voices raised in defence of their authenticity would grow feebler and fewer.

Has Montefiore's prophecy been fulfilled? How stand the verses today? It seems to me eminently worth-while to take a look at what the critics have been saying about them during the last quarter of a century.

I

To begin with, I think we must say that the attack made by Harnack on the 'canonical' text has broken down. It was always a pretty precarious case he had to argue, since (1) the weight of the MS evidence was solidly behind the received text, and (2) the Church Fathers, on whom Harnack strongly relied, were often inaccurate quoters. Still, Harnack's argument, backed as it was by his great patristic learning, did sound impressive when he made it. He believed that the *Jubelruf*, as Huck's Synopsis calls it, came from Q, but he invoked the evidence of second and third century Fathers to argue that the form of the saying in Luke was originally different, and that what stood in Q was this:

All things have been delivered to me by the Father, and no one *knew* the Father but the Son, and anyone to whom the Son revealed him.

In other words, he believed that the clause about the Father's knowledge of the Son had been interpolated at an early date from Matthew into Luke, and that the earliest version of Luke had 'knew' (*egnō*) not 'knows' (*ginōskei*), in the clause about the Son's knowledge of the Father. In this shortened form the saying was an authentic logion of Jesus.

Seldom has one textual critic been more ably answered by another as

[1] *The Synoptic Gospels*, vol. II, 169, 186.

Harnack was by Chapman.[1] The patristic evidence showed, said Chapman, that every patristic instance of *egnō* was in Matthew, not Luke (as Harnack had averred), and that the patristic variations in the order of the two clauses in v. 27 were almost certainly due to quotation from memory. (How hard it is to quote this verse accurately from memory, we all of us know by practical experience.)

Consequently, anyone nowadays who wishes, on textual grounds, to excise the clause about the Father's knowledge of the Son must answer Chapman's argument. Nor is this all: in the intervening years other and cogent arguments for the canonical text have been advanced.

Thus, it has been recently and persuasively argued that the usual order of the clauses in v. 27 constitutes the *lectio difficilior*, since it makes the Son a bigger mystery than the Father.[2]

Further, it has been well contended that to excise the clause about the Father's knowledge of the Son ruins the theological sense of the passage. The clause supplies the presupposition of the one about the son's knowledge of the Father. It is the Father's prevenient knowledge of the Son which makes meaningful the Son's claim to know the Father.[3]

Lastly, the reading *egnō* may plausibly be explained as an assimilation to the preceding aorists.

We therefore conclude that at least vv. 25-27 stood in Q, probably in their Matthean form, since Luke's indirect questions ('Who the Son is', 'Who the Father is') look like deliberate attempts to improve Matthew's blunt accusatives.

Let us now address ourselves to the question of the genuineness and interpretation of the three strophes in our passage—vv. 25-26, 27 and 28-30.

[1] *Journal of Theological Studies* X (1909), 552 ff.
[2] So T. Zahn, A. Schlatter, J. Schniewind, J. Bieneck and O. Cullmann. The text favoured by Harnack (and T. W. Manson) looks like an attempt to ease the 'difficulty'. Yet the idea which it stresses—that God is inaccessible to human thought—is typically Greek and contrary to the tenor of the New Testament. Bieneck (*Sohn Gottes*, 82) thinks the 'divergent' text was due to the influence of Marcion with his doctrine of 'the unknown God'. On the other hand, the 'canonical' text consists (*a*) with the Synoptic view of Jesus' Sonship, bringing us face to face with the *Mysterium Christi*, and (*b*) with that 'lowliness' of Jesus which was the very soul of his filial obedience—
        The kingdom that I seek
        Is Thine; so let the way
        That leads to it be Thine—
and had been prophesied for the Servant of the Lord (Isa. 52.14; 53.2 f.). His lot was to be misunderstood by men, and in the Gospel event even his disciples deserted, denied and betrayed him.
[3] Dalman (*Words of Jesus*, 283) declares the two clauses in v. 27 inseparable, and says that they are an oriental way of 'expressing the reciprocity of intimate understanding'.

II
Strophe I: Matt. 11.25 f. (Luke 10.21)

I thank thee, Father, Lord of heaven and earth,
That thou hast hidden these things from the wise and clever,
And hast revealed them to the simple (*nēpiois*)
Yes, Father, for such was thy gracious will.

Few scholars nowadays dispute the genuineness of this strophe. Why should they? It contains so many marks of authenticity—its poetic structure, the *exhomologeomai* formula, its Old Testament echoes (Isa. 29.16; Ps. 19.7), the word 'Father' probably concealing an original Aramaic *Abba*, the apparent harshness of the 'Thank God for their unbelief', a typical Aramaic periphrasis[1] in the last line, and the congruency of the strophe with the known course of Christ's Ministry.

If we could fix its original *Sitz im Leben Jesu*, our problems of interpretation would be greatly eased. Matthew locates it in the midst of the Galilean Ministry, setting it after Christ's 'Woes' on the Galilean Cities. Luke attaches it to the Return of the Seventy and the report of their success. It is conceivable that in both Gospels the setting is eschatological and that *tauta*, 'these things', refers to these eschatological events. We can then say that the eschatological 'awareness' implied by *tauta* is coupled with the 'knowledge' which the Father has delivered to the Son and which the Son has of the Father. This juxtaposition of insight into the eschatological nature of events and intimate knowledge between Father and Son has parallels, as W. D. Davies has shown,[2] in the Dead Sea Scrolls.

On the other hand, this passage may be, like so many others in the Gospels, one which has come down to us without a special setting. If this is so, and 'scientific guesses' are permitted, we may follow both T. W.[3] and William Manson[4] in placing it after Caesarea Philippi when increasing evidence of the disciples' growing faith may have moved Jesus to draw back a corner of the veil which concealed the last secret of his own spiritual life.

In any case, *tauta* must refer, in one form or another, to the secret of the presence of the Kingdom which was the burden of Jesus' preaching. And since it was to the disciples, and them only, that Jesus spoke of his knowledge of Abba, Father,[5] *tauta* may refer, more particularly (as

---

[1] *hoti houtōs eudokia egeneto emprosthen sou.*
[2] *Harvard Theological Review* 46 (1953), 137 f.
[3] *The Teaching of Jesus*, 110.   [4] *Jesus the Messiah*, 108.
[5] T. W. Manson, op. cit., 102.

Bieneck[1] has argued), to the secret of his own unique Sonship. If so, we have an excellent connection between Strophes I and II.

The meaning of the strophe itself is tolerably clear. As 'the wise and clever' (Isa. 29.14) are doubtless the official custodians of Israel's wisdom, the Scribes, so the 'simple' (*nēpia* in the LXX renders *petha'im*: Pss. 19.7; 116.6) are the child-like to whom the Kingdom belongs (Mark 10.18 f.; Matt. 18.3)—in short, his circle of disciples. Not to the sophisticated but to the simple—not to those proudly sure of their title to 'the very shape of knowledge and truth' (Rom. 2.20) but to those unskilled in scribe-lore as babes—has his teaching come as the Divine revelation which it is. But in this apparent miscarriage—this 'awriness' of things —Jesus discerns the gracious purpose of the Almighty Father and thanks him for it.

Does Jesus give thanks for the Scribes' unbelief? Then surely we have to recognize here a Semitic *façon de parler*. We might have said that, in the providence of God, 'pride of knowledge' had brought its nemesis, its fall.[2] In any case, a revelation accessible to 'babes' is *ipso facto* accessible to all—even Scribes, if they are prepared to become as little children. We know of one proud pupil of Gamaliel who did so. In fact, St Paul may well have known this saying, as Harnack thought he did. 'Whenever I read I Cor. 1.19, 21,' he said,[3] 'I am ever again struck by the coincidence here, both in thought and vocabulary, with our saying, though all of course has passed through the crucible of Paul's mind.'

III
Strophe II: Matt. *11.27* (*Luke 10.22*)

All things have been delivered to me by my Father:
And no one knows the Son but the Father;
Neither does any know the Father but the Son,
And any one to whom the Son chooses to reveal him.

The connection with the preceding verses seems logical and natural. As Strophe I gives thanks for the revelation and its recipients—not the wise but the simple—so Strophe II declares the way by which the revelation comes—from the Father through the Son.

But with this verse we reach the real storm-centre. Forty or fifty years

[1] *Sohn Gottes*, 85.
[2] If this logion smacks of Divine determinism, we get the other side of the medal—the stress on human free-will—in Jesus' parable of the Great Supper (Luke 14.16-24). Here, addressing the professedly religious in the land, Jesus says in effect: 'If you find yourselves outside the Kingdom, you have only yourselves to blame, since you have refused God's invitation.'
[3] *The Sayings of Jesus*, 301, n. 1.

ago when *Religiongeschichte* dominated our *Neutestamentlers'* thinking, men like Norden, Bousset and Klostermann were quite sure Jesus could not have uttered it. Three main charges were levelled:

1. Jesus could not have made the absolute claim in this verse.
2. The saying has a tell-tale Johannine ring.
3. Both form and content show it to be a Hellenistic 'revelation word'.

These were never impressive reasons, and in the last thirty years they have worn decidedly thin. Let us look at them one by one.

Mark 13.32 (one of Schmiedel's 'foundation pillars') provides a precise parallel to the absolute Father-Son usage of this verse. But there is enough evidence elsewhere in the Synoptic tradition (Luke 2.49; Mark 1.11; 12.6 plus Jesus' unique invocation of God as *Abba*[1]) to make it quite credible that Jesus could have styled himself 'the Son' *simpliciter*, as later theologians like Paul and John believed he did. Moreover, the verse but sets the capstone on much else in the Synoptic tradition suggestive of what Vincent Taylor has called 'the Divine Consciousness of Jesus'.[2]

Nor does the second charge stand up any more firmly. That the saying resembles several sayings in John (e.g. 3.35; 10.15) is ungainsayable. But this is no reason at all for condemning it unless we make it a canon of criticism that any saying in the Synoptics with a parallel in John must *ipso facto* be spurious. The precise opposite might indeed be argued: that if we find in John a logion with parallels in the Synoptics, John either depends on the Synoptics or else draws upon an independent tradition. As everybody knows, scholars now increasingly believe not only that John was independent of the Synoptics but that he may even have used a special sayings-source—a kind of Johannine Q. In the

---

[1] Jesus' use of the word *Abba* (a diminutive form from children's speech) in addressing God has no parallel in Jewish literature. 'His meaning,' says Jeremias (*TLZ* 1954, No. 4, 213), 'is shown by an analysis of Matt. 11.27 (Luke 10.22)—a logion quite Semitic in character—to be Christological. This means: the word *Abba* is the most important feature in the esoteric message of Jesus.'

[2] *The Person of Christ*, 156 f. In the Synoptics we are confronted by One who not only opposed his 'sovereign I' to the dictates of the Law of Moses but declared that the supreme organ of God's will on earth, Israel, would be wrecked on its attitude to himself: one who chose for himself the high and mysterious title of 'Son of man' and promised God's Kingdom to those who attached themselves to his person: one who never prayed with his disciples (though he often prayed for them) but who solemnly affirmed that on their acceptance or rejection of himself men's eternal destiny would depend: one who appeared among men as the Divine Forgiveness incarnate and declared that his death as the Servant of the Lord would ransom a countless multitude from their sins. Such a one stands not with men before God but between God and men and is amply entitled to make the mediatorial claim of Matt. 11.27.

present state of Johannine studies, then, it will simply not do to imagine that by murmuring the word 'Johannine' we have settled, negatively, the problem of the genuineness of Matt. 11.27.

Still less is it permissible to dismiss the saying lightly as a Hellenistic 'revelation word' (Bultmann). The Hellenistic parallels to it raked up by Reitzenstein and Co. were never very impressive,[1] and in the last two decades the discovery of the Dead Sea Scrolls has completely altered the picture. So large a role does 'knowledge' play in the Scrolls that it is quite 'unnecessary to go outside a Jewish milieu to account for our passage'.[2] Not Hellenism but Hosea[3] (a book well known to Jesus)—not pagan *gnōsis* but Old Testament—and Qumran—*da'th Elohim* supplies the likeliest background to the supreme 'I-Thou' relationship of Matt. 11.27. On this point recent scholars (Schniewind, T. W. Manson, Taylor, Bieneck, Dupont and Fuller) speak with almost one voice.

To be sure, no such *exclusive* claim is ever made in the Old Testament. But if the Old Testament yields no precise parallel to Matt. 11.27, we should not expect to find one. We are in the presence of a unique Person making a unique claim. But certainly not a surprising one if Jesus knew himself to represent Israel—called of old 'my Son' by Hosea—and to be the Fulfiller of her hope.

We conclude that if men reject this logion, they reject it not because they have proved it a Hellenistic revelation word, or because its Johannine sound condemns it, but because they have made up their minds, *a priori*, that the Jesus of history could not have made such a claim.

Now for the interpretation.

'All things (*panta*) have been delivered (*paredothē*) to me by my Father.' The debate about the meaning of *panta* is not over, for some moderns (Schniewind, Dupont, etc.) still take it to mean 'all power', quoting Dan. 7.14 and Matt. 28.18. But most modern scholars prefer 'all knowledge'—all the revelation needed for his task—and with sound reason:

(*a*) Jesus proceeds to speak, and speak exclusively, of the knowledge of God; (*b*) since Jesus was not yet 'glorified', the idea of universal power is not yet relevant; (*c*) the very word *paredothē* suggests a contrast with the *paradosis* of the Scribes (cf. Mark 7.3, 9) who are clearly in view

---

[1] E.g. the Hymn to Echnaton or the London Magical Papyrus. ('I know you, Hermes, and you know me. I am you and you are I.' *Gnōsis theou* here is not a personal relationship—as in Matt. 11.27—but an absorption into deity.)

[2] W. D. Davies, op. cit., 139.

[3] See G. A. Smith's magnificent chapter on 'the knowledge of God' in *The Book of the Twelve Prophets*, vol. I, 318-32.

in the first and last strophes. Their 'tradition' or 'handing down' was from man to man. *Per contra*, the 'handing down' here was directly from God. *Panta* therefore means the complete revelation of God's (and his) saving purpose: 'All I need to know for my task has been taught me by the Father' (P. T. Forsyth).[1]

The next two clauses show why Jesus believes himself qualified to reveal that purpose. His competence, he says, is grounded in an exclusive and reciprocal relationship between the Father and himself, the Son—

> No one knows the Son but the Father,
> Neither does any know the Father but the Son.

The order of the clauses answers to the Old Testament concept of *da'ath Elohim*. In the prophet's view, if man is ever to know God, God must first know man. And it is because of the Father's prevenient knowledge of himself, that Jesus can claim that he knows the Father as none other does. Here of course we are in the realm of ultimate mystery. The secret of the Father remains with the Son alone. No man knew, or knows, why the Father chose Jesus of Nazareth.

Even so, we are not debarred from indicating what Jesus meant by 'knowing' God; and it is not to Hellenism (still less to modern occidental ideas of knowledge) but to the Old Testament that we must look for our clue. What is meant here is not theological learning but a personal 'I-Thou' relation engaging heart and mind and will—a relation initiated and sustained by the Father, and complemented and fulfilled by Jesus' own filial response of obedience and love—a response writ large in the Gospel record from the Wilderness to Gethsemane. If 'communion with God' is our best English equivalent, we must interpret that communion (as the Old Testament does) in an existential and ethical way. Finally, unique though that communion is, it is one into which Jesus claims to be able to lead others—

> And any one to whom the Son chooses to reveal him.

In this strophe, then, Jesus claims that he is both to God and man what no other can be. He is the Son who alone knows the Father, and he is the mediator through whom alone this personal knowledge of the Father —this 'I-Thou' relation promised for the last days in Jeremiah's great prophecy (Jer. 31.34)—comes to men. If in John 14.6 Jesus claims to be 'the true and living way', and the only one, the claim finds solid root in

---

[1] *The Person and Place of Jesus Christ,* 112.

the Synoptic tradition. It is worth adding that, in the judgment of A. Schweitzer and P. T. Forsyth, this verse implies in Jesus the consciousness of pre-existence.[1]

IV
Strophe III: Matt. 11.28-30 (Om. Luke)

Come to me, all who labour and are heavy laden,
And I will give you rest.
Take my yoke upon you, and learn from me,
For I am gentle and lowly in heart
And you will find rest (anapausis) for your souls.
For my yoke is easy, and my burden is light.

Thirty or forty years ago radical criticism unhesitatingly judged these wonderful words unauthentic. One count against them was that they apparently did not stand in Q.[2] Those were the days when the Two-Document Theory dominated our thinking on the Synoptics, and anything which could not be shown to derive from Q lay under deep suspicion. This was a highly doubtful assumption, as we now realize; for, on this reasoning, about half of Christ's parables, including many of his greatest, would at once be branded with a reputation of dubious historicity; which is plainly absurd.

Oddly enough, some who took this view (like Norden) were convinced that Matt. 11.25-30 formed an indivisible whole. Prima facie, this seems unlikely, for the last strophe suggests that it was originally spoken not to disciples but to outsiders. Nevertheless, it was a sound instinct which persuaded them to hold the three strophes together. In form, the Great Invitation resembles the Great Thanksgiving.[3] Moreover, it is hard not to feel 'an inward affinity' between the first two strophes and the last one. The third strophe does undeniably make the most excellent sense where it stands in Matthew. William Manson[4] saw this: 'Because Jesus is the unique revealer of God in his teaching,' he wrote, 'He holds the secret of life and peace for all who turn to Him.' And Schniewind was of the same mind.[5] We are therefore warranted in studying all three strophes together.

---

[1] A. Schweitzer, Geschichte der Leben Jesu Forschung, 310; Forsyth, op. cit., iii.
[2] This is not certain: it may be, as Dibelius thought, that they did, but that Luke omitted them because he deemed them inappropriate to his context (the Return of the Seventy). See From Tradition to Gospel, 279, n. 1.
[3] In the latter the first thought is for the revelation itself, and then the revelation is said to be mediated by the Son. So, in the Great Invitation, there is first a general offer of rest, and then it is said that the rest is to be had by acceptance of his yoke.
[4] Jesus the Messiah, 73.   [5] Matthäus, 155.

Now let us come back to the question of authenticity. If our inability to prove that Strophe III stood in Q should not prejudice a verdict on its genuineness, no more should the fact that it contains echoes of Ecclesiasticus 51. This book, which was written in Hebrew in Jerusalem about two hundred years before, was very popular among the Jews and may well have been known to Jesus.

When we examine the authenticity of this last strophe, much in it has a clear ring of authenticity.

Semitic originals seem to glimmer through the Greek. To the evidence of Semitic word-play discerned by Meyer,[1] we may add the knowledge of the Hebrew Bible evident in the echoes from Ecclesiasticus and Jeremiah.

Next, the promise of *anapausis* ('relief': New English Bible) to the heavy-laden is entirely in the spirit of One who condemned the Scribes for 'loading men with burdens hard to bear' (Luke 11.46; Matt. 23.4).

Third, the self-description, 'I am gentle and lowly in heart' echoes the description of the Servant in Isa. 42.2 f. and 53.1 ff. and is apparently confirmed in II Cor. 10.1 where Paul appeals to 'the meekness and gentleness of Christ' as to something familiar and well-known.

Fourth, it is an evidence of primary tradition that the yoke of Jesus is declared to be 'easy' and his burden 'light'. We know that some of his first followers did not always find them so.

Add up all this evidence, and it becomes hard to believe that this logion is not substantially genuine. This is the verdict of most recent scholars.[2] For myself, I agree with the famous judgment of Walter Pater on it: there is numinous mystery about it, and if I am asked to choose between regarding it as a community creation and a genuine word of Jesus, my mind is quickly made up.

Otto's view,[3] that we have here a straight quotation from Ecclus 51 and that Jesus is speaking *in persona Sapientiae*, goes much too far. What we have is not straight quotation but some echoes of Ecclus 51 plus a sentence from Jer. 6.16 (Hebrew, not LXX). And the important thing to note is how Jesus adapts Ben Sira's words for his own purpose, turning them round completely.

Ben Sira, inviting men to the study of the Law,[4] says: 'Put your necks

---

[1] *Jesu Muttersprache*, 84.
[2] Otto, Schniewind, Schlatter, Bieneck, W. Manson, T. W. Manson, etc.
[3] *The Kingdom of God and the Son of Man*, 137 ff.
[4] T. W. Manson, in *The Sayings of Jesus*, 186, observes: 'Under all this poetical eloquence [Ecclus 51.23-27] it is plain enough what the author is commending: it is the study of the Law.' (The 'house of instruction' is the *Beth ha-Midrash*.) The contrast in Jesus' saying is between the yoke of the Law and

D

under her [the Law's] yoke, and let your soul accept her burden. See I have worked but little and found much rest.' The preacher of the Law runs true to type: his confidence in works of Law remains unshaken.

Jesus says the precise opposite. To those burdened by the Law's demands he promises 'relief'; and for the Scribes' heavy yoke he promises his own 'kindly' one, the yoke of a Kingdom in which Abba Father is sovereign, the 'rest' which is the peace of that new relationship with God which he knows himself uniquely qualified to mediate.

It is a promise whose truth was classically validated by the experience of his greatest apostle. A generation later, in his greatest letter, Paul was to record how, when he groaned under the Law's burden, he found relief by accepting the Great Invitation. Through Christ the mediator he found the longed-for new relationship with God—one of sonship, not of slavery—because through *the* Son he had access to the Father. And if it involved a new law—'the law of Christ' (Gal. 6.2)—this law, by the testimony of his own Christian life, was no burden because he had put his neck under Christ's yoke and had the enabling power of his Spirit.

It only remains for me to add, as my last word, that I do not think Montefiore's prophecy has been fulfilled.

the yoke of the Kingdom. In discipleship to himself men will find rest for their souls. This is what Ben Sira claims he has got from the Law. So Rengstorf, *s.v.* *zygon* in Kittel's *TWNT* II, 902: 'It is a contrast between Messiah's yoke and the yoke of Law-religion. . . . The promise of the saying is that he who commits himself to Jesus [i.e., enters the Kingdom] . . . will find access to the Father— an access not the result of human achievement but the gift of Jesus in his work and person.'

V

THE INTERPRETATION OF
THE PARABLES

I T is almost incredible yet true that from the Apostolic Age to the end of the nineteenth century the parables of Jesus were regularly misinterpreted. This misinterpretation stemmed from one erroneous assumption, that the parables were allegories.

Now the basic difference between an allegory (like Paul's picture of the Christian Warrior in Ephesians 6 or *The Pilgrim's Progress*) and a parable is this: whereas in the allegory each detail is a separate metaphor with a significance of its own which has to be discovered, the parable exists to enforce one point. Thus the parable of The Prodigal Son, which we ought to call the parable of The Gracious Father (since he is the central figure in it), proclaims one truth—the free forgiveness of God to penitent sinners—but watch what happened when so eminent an Early Church Father as Tertullian expounded it. The elder son is the Jew, the younger the Christian. The patrimony, of which the younger son claimed his share, is that knowledge of God a man has by his birthright. The citizen in the far country to whom he hired his services is the Devil. The robe bestowed on the penitent Prodigal is that sonship from which Adam fell, as the ensuing feast is the Lord's Supper. We may at least be grateful that he made no attempt to identify the fatted calf!

But even Tertullian's ingenuity pales before that of the great Augustine when he got busy on the Good Samaritan. You remember his equations? The 'certain man' who went down from Jerusalem to Jericho is Adam, Jerusalem representing the heavenly city of peace from which he fell, and Jericho our human mortality to which he went. The robbers are the Devil and his angels, who stripped Adam of his immortality. The priest and the Levite who passed by on the other side are the priesthood and ministry of the Old Testament who could not save. Who is the Good Samaritan but Christ himself? The binding up of the traveller's wounds is the restraint of sin, while the oil poured in is the comfort of hope. The beast is the flesh in which Christ came to earth;

the inn is the Church; the inn-keeper the Apostle Paul; and the two pence, the commandments of love. *C'est pittoresque—mais ce n'est pas histoire!*

Yes, we smile at it, but the book many of our grandfathers used, Trench on the Parables (1841) does the same thing (if not quite so badly) and I have no doubt that the method still has its practitioners.

The great protest against all this misguided subtlety was made in 1899 by Adolf Jülicher in his *Die Gleichnisreden Jesu*, a book which deserved but never found an English translator. The parables, Jülicher insisted, are not allegorical cryptograms to be spelled out, point after point, by an ingenious exegesis. They have one point, and one point only. On that point the whole comparison focuses, and the various details in the story, which give it an air of verisimilitude, are but feathers to wing the arrow to its mark.

That Jülicher was fundamentally right, nobody nowadays doubts. The only question to be asked is, Has he not, like most pioneers, over-played his hand a little? Do the parables of Jesus *never* contain allegory? Is there not a veiled reference to Jesus as the 'bridegroom' in the little parable of The Sons of the Bridechamber? And, clearer still, in the tale of The Wicked Vinedressers is not the Owner of the Vineyard God, his servants, the prophets, and the Beloved Son, Christ himself? In short, we must not let the shade of Jülicher affright us from admitting some allegorical elements in the parables, more especially when we know that allegory formed part of the cultural heritage of Jesus? (The Old Testament contains a number of allegories, and we know that the rabbis used them.)

But if the parable exists to make one point, what kind of point is it? It was in this part of the enquiry that Jülicher having insisted on the one point, went on to miss it completely. His capital error was to make the parables teach *moral commonplaces*. If you turn to him asking what is the point of the parable of The Talents, the answer you get is: 'A reward is only earned by performance.' Similarly the story of The Unjust Steward teaches: 'Wise use of the present is the condition of future happiness.' The point of the Rich Fool is that 'even the wealthiest of men depends wholly on the power and mercy of God'. And so on.

You can guess what his final picture was like. The Jesus who emerges from Jülicher's researches is a typically Liberal Jesus who goes about indoctrinating men in moral truth by the deft use of picturesque parables. But is this the real Jesus? And would men have ever bothered to

crucify a Galilean Tusitala who told pleasant stories to enforce pruden-
tial platitudes? Of course they wouldn't.

But if Jülicher had left the task of interpretation half done, he had
cleared the way for the next and revolutionary advance which came
thirty-six years later. Need I say that I am referring to C. H. Dodd's
Parables of the Kingdom (1935)? I can still remember the thrill with
which I read that book. Dodd, if I may adapt Lowell's words, cut the
cables and gave me a glimpse of blue waters. And I should agree with
Joachim Jeremias, who, a dozen years later (1947), was to dot the i's and
stroke the t's of Dodd's exposition, that it is unthinkable there should
ever be any retreat from Dodd's essential insights. What then did
Dodd and Jeremias do which Jülicher had not done? *They put the
parables back into their true setting, which is the ministry of Jesus seen as
the great eschatological act of God in which he visited and redeemed his
people.* But are not the parables already in their true setting? Some are,
but by no means all of them. We must remember that in the period of
the oral tradition—roughly, the generation AD 30-60—many of the
parables circulated as separate units, and inevitably their original settings were often forgotten and lost,[1] so that the Church was forced to
give them new settings and applications. I will take three examples.
Beyond any doubt on Jesus' lips the parable of The Lost Sheep was
aimed at Pharisees and others who complained that Jesus welcomed
sinners. This is its setting in Luke, and its true one; but turn the parable
up in Matthew and you will find that it is there addressed to the
disciples and has become a call to faithful pastorship. Or consider the
parable of The Defendant which occurs in both Matthew and Luke.
When Jesus told this parable, it was a summons to Israel to repent
before it was too late in face of the great crisis which was the coming of
God's reign. 'Come to terms with God before his judgment falls on
you!' But in Matthew's Sermon on the Mount it has become a *moral*
rule on the importance of reconciliation. Now it says: 'Don't let your
quarrel with your brother take you the length of the law-court.' Or
consider the parable of The Talents found in Matthew, with its variant
version of The Pounds in Luke, so that we might call it the parable of
Money in Trust. As it stands now in the Gospels, it reads like a summons to be faithful in view of the imminence of our Lord's Second
Coming. But when Jesus spoke the parable, he was addressing the
religious leaders of Jewry, to whom so much had been entrusted, and

---

[1] Cf. Matt. 13, where seven parables have been collected together, their
original settings having been lost.

warning them that the Day of God's reckoning with them was at hand. And it was, as history shows.

Once you recognize these things, it becomes possible to restore the parables to their original settings and see them against their proper historical background. What is it? It is what we have learned to call 'realized eschatology'. Now don't let us quarrel over the word 'realized' —substitute if you like, the word 'inaugurated'; but this is undoubtedly the true backcloth against which the parables of Jesus become pregnant with point and meaning, weapons of war, if you like, in the campaign of the Kingdom of God against the Kingdom of the Devil. You can then arrange them in groups, so that the Kingdom themes which Jesus meant them to illustrate stand out, and the essential notes of the Galilean gospel ring out vividly and memorably.

Jeremias proposes eight such groupings, but I think we can get along pretty well with four:

(1) First, *How the Kingdom Comes and Grows*. Here the twin parables of The New Patch on the Old Garment and The New Wine in the Old Wineskins proclaim the utter newness of the Kingdom and the folly of all attempts to accommodate it to the old order. (This is the point Paul was later to develop in his contrast between the Law and the gospel.) Four parables tell us how the Kingdom comes and grows; with certainty and to great endings, say the two parables of The Mustard Seed and The Leaven; quietly but irresistibly, says the parable of The Seed Growing Secretly; and in spite of all failures, yielding an abundant harvest, says that story of a farmer's fortunes which we call The Sower. But Jesus does not confine himself to images from agriculture. He sees the Kingdom as God's Great Feast, to which the invitation goes out, 'Come, for all things are now ready.' Or as a great warfare against the Kingdom of the Devil in which he, the Messiah, spearheads the attack (The Divided Kingdom and The Strong Man Despoiled). He compares it to a seine net which catches all kinds of fish. So the gospel of the Kingdom makes its appeal to all and sundry but in the process sifts worthy and unworthy, by their response to its claims and challenges.

(2) The second group of parables may be entitled *The Blessings of the Kingdom: God's Mercy for Sinners*.

None of the groups takes us so near to the heart of the Good News as this one,[1] in which the grace of God is the dominant note. We hear it in the parable of The Labourers in the Vineyard which says: 'The rewards of the Kingdom are not measured by man's desert but by God's

---

[1] Jeremias calls it 'the gospel within the Gospels'.

grace.' This in answer to the criticism that Jesus opened the Kingdom to publicans and harlots. For the strange thing is that this group of parables were all spoken to his *critics* in defence of the gospel. I have mentioned The Lost Sheep. Its companion parable, The Lost Coin, spoken to Pharisees who complained that Jesus 'received sinners', proclaims the same truth: 'If a man will be at such pains to recover his lost property, how much more will God to save his wandering children? This is what I, as God's Representative, am doing.' The same is true of the greatest parable of all, The Prodigal Son. The simplest explanation is that the father represents God, the elder brother the complaining Pharisees, and the younger brother the publicans and sinners. It puts in terms of moving human relations the supreme truth which Paul borrowed law-court language to express; 'the God who justifies the ungodly'. Finally, to this same gospel of God's mercy to sinners belongs The Pharisee and the Publican. Speaking to all friends of the elder brother (and they still exist!) Jesus says in it: 'God rejects the self-righteous and welcomes the despairing sinner. This is what the Almighty is like, and how he is acting through me.'

(3) The third group of parables describes: *Discipleship in the Kingdom.*

To be a disciple of Jesus is to be in the Kingdom, since Jesus himself embodies, and is, the Kingdom. Such parables suggest the meaning of true discipleship. His call for disciples we hear in the parable of The Harvest and the Labourers. Before men decide, they must count well the cost, say the twin parables of The Tower Builder and The Warring King. But to win its riches is something worth any sacrifice, say the parables of The Hid Treasure and The Precious Pearl. In the companion parables of The Importunate Widow and The Friend at Midnight, Jesus calls for men with a faith which refuses to take 'No' for an answer and ever expects great things from God. True disciples, as men in whom God has kindled his light, are, like Isaiah's Servant, to be 'a light to lighten the Gentiles' (Lamp and Bushel, and cf. Matt. 5.14); but they must beware: as old Israel lost its savour, so too may God's new Israel (Savourless Salt). Let them be men known for their abounding forgiveness (The Unmerciful Servant) and for their deeds rather than their fine professions (The Two Builders and The Tree and the Fruit).

(4) Finally, we come to a very important group of parables all dealing with *The Crisis of the Kingdom.*

Here we need to remember that Jesus saw his ministry, which was the inauguration of the Reign of God, moving on to a supreme crisis in

God's dealings with his people, a crisis which would involve not only the Messiah's death and victory and the rise of a New Israel but also the destruction of the Jewish nation and Temple. Against such a background all the parables which deal in Zero Hour and General Emergency become luminous. In some he warns the Jewish people against the time of God's visitation (The Playing Children, Weather Signs, The Talents) and calls Israel to repent before it is too late (The Defendant, The Barren Fig Tree, The Closed Door); in others he seeks to 'alert' them to the Great Emergency (The Porter, The Burglar, The Ten Virgins).[1]

But, alas, Israel did not know the time of her visitation or the things that belonged unto her peace, and the great drama moved to its climax.

So the Son of man, the Speaker of the parables and the central Figure in the drama, marched on Jerusalem where, on an April morning in the year AD 30, the crisis culminated in a Crucifixion outside the city wall, and, three days later, in an Empty Tomb. One great parable, which is half allegory, preserves for us his final warning to the Jewish leaders— the parable of The Wicked Vinedressers. It is 'Love's last appeal' to a rebellious people. No full-length parable survives to tell us how the Messiah conceived of the purpose of his dying; but the gospel tradition preserves three parables in miniature which take us some way into the secret: the sayings about The Cup, The Baptism, and The Ransom. The Messiah was drinking the Cup of the Lord's wrath; he was undergoing a Baptism of blood whereby others might be cleansed; as the Servant Messiah, he was giving his life to ransom 'the many'.

By his death and resurrection, the Kingdom of God, which had been the theme of all his parables, 'came with power'; the Holy Spirit descended on the waiting disciples, and the new People of God, which is the Christian Church, was born.

And now, by way of epilogue, let me raise the question: How does all this affect us who have to preach from the Bible and would fain make effective use of the parables?

One thing is clear. Much of what the scholars are telling us runs counter to interpretations of the parables long current in the Church. Must all our sermons embodying such interpretations be forthwith consigned to the waste-paper basket? My answer would be 'No'—if the sermons have authentic spiritual value of their own. For a true Word of the Lord may be drawn from a parable of Jesus, even though it depends on a turn of meaning not in our Lord's mind when he told it.

---

[1] Possibly The Unjust Steward should be included in this group: 'This knave knew how to act in an emergency; so must you in a much greater one!'

But if we mean to claim his authority for such utterances of ours, let us be sure that they really represent his teaching. 'Here', as Dr G. H. Boobyer has said, 'Biblical scholarship rightly exercises an important function, for the spirits of the prophets should be subject not only to the prophets but also, to some extent, to the professors!'

This said, let me suggest that the scholars' findings on the parables mean two things:

(1) No more capricious allegorizing of the parables; and (2) No more employment of them simply as pegs for moralizing sermons.

Positively, the new approach to the parables means that, when we decide to preach from one, our first task should be to discover what our Lord meant when he first uttered it. There we must begin, though we must not stop there. But someone may say: 'If the true setting-in-life of the parables is the historic crisis of AD 28-30, when God came in Christ's ministry and mission, have they any relevance for AD 1962?'

Most certainly they have. For if the parables let us into the secret of what the coming of Christ and the Kingdom meant to his contemporaries, by the same token do they interpret for us our own experience to whom God still comes in the crises of the twentieth century. Says C. H. Dodd: 'The historical crisis of the Gospels is re-enacted in the crises that come upon men and nations. God in His Kingdom, power and glory, confronts us too with blessing and judgment, with challenge and opportunity. In such situations the parables leap out of their historical settings and speak to our condition.'

Lest this sound too vague and general to be helpful, let me remind you that the greatest of Christ's parables have about them a timeless quality. The parable of The Good Samaritan never ceases to pose its question: 'Who is my neighbour?' and its true answer is given in lives like those of Grenfell of Labrador, Kagawa of Japan and Schweitzer of Lambarene. So, too, with such parables as The Prodigal Son, The Sower, The Rich Man and Lazarus, The Pharisee and the Publican. If a man cannot preach the Word of God to this generation from such parables he ought not to be in the Christian ministry.

Other parables, like those in the fourth group, which are more specifically related to the crisis of AD 28-30, may seem to pose a harder problem. But consider their main themes. Do they not call on us, as they did on Jesus' own generation, to 'discern the signs of the times', to realize that God still visits men in judgment and blessing, and to know that the constant duty of Christians is to repent and hear what God the Lord is saying to them amid all the chaos of this twentieth century?

Yes, the parables still speak, if we will but hear our Lord with understanding and translate his words into modern terms. Read Henry Scott Holland on The Sower, J. S. Whale on the Friend at Midnight, or J. S. Stewart on 'Love's Last Appeal', and you will be in no doubt about it. By prayful study and with the guidance of the Spirit, we too may hear what God in Christ has to say to us in these old, old stories and find in them light to lead us through these dark and dangerous days:

> Bewildered, dejected and prone to despair,
> To Him as at first do we turn and beseech.
> Our ears are all open! Give heed to our prayer.
> O Son of man, teach.

VI

RECENT TRENDS IN
JOHANNINE STUDIES

W AS there ever a book which inspired such a flood of writing about it
as the Gospel according to St John? Nor does the flood show any signs
of abating. The last decade has produced its own quota of notable books
on the Gospel; and whatever the 'sixties' may hold for the world in
general, we may safely prophesy that they will add to Johannine
bibliography.

But do all these books really increase our understanding of this
Gospel whose words, as Luther said, are so simple yet so inexpressible?
Or are our savants just ringing the changes on the old issues and
darkening counsel with learned words?

Whatever the cynical may say, it seems to us that in recent years the
Johannine debate has taken some very interesting turns. Our scholars
now expend far less time and ink than the men of the last generation
in re-shuffling the leaves of the Gospel to secure an allegedly better
order or in trying to separate off a hypothetical *Grundschrift* from the
work of various redactors. Finding no certainty on the question of
authorship, they have concentrated on the book itself, its background
and its theology, with results that seem highly promising for the
future.

Paradoxically enough, it has sometimes been *Alttestamentlers* who
have given the debate its most stimulating turns. First, it was C. F.
Burney, then C. C. Torrey, and finally W. F. Albright. Of all the excellent essays in the *Festschrift* for C. H. Dodd none has excited more
comment than Albright's essay on the Fourth Gospel.[1] In what follows
we propose to develop some of his suggestions and to combine them
with the fruits of other recent researchers.

The trends of our title concern the language of the Gospel, its topography, its background, and its historical traditions. Let us see where
we stand on these matters in 1960.

---

[1] *The Background of the New Testament and its Eschatology*, 153-71.

I

First, we can be tolerably sure (thanks to Schlatter, Burney, Torrey, Driver, and Black) that St John's Greek reveals an unmistakable Aramaic accent.

Every reader of the Gospel remembers how St John transliterates Aramaic words like Cephas and Gabbatha and adds a Greek translation. This in itself implies some knowledge of Aramaic. But the Aramaic quality of John's Greek is not a matter of single words only but of syntax, idiom, and general style.

Consider, for example, his fondness for parataxis, i.e. the setting side by side of complete sentences with main verbs instead of using subordinate clauses. Your good Greek writer prefers to use one main verb and surround it with subordinate clauses. But parataxis is a prime feature of Hebrew and Aramaic style, and it is significant how very fond St John is of it. 'He spat . . . and made . . . and put . . . and said' (John 9.6 f.). This is the kind of thing we find in many of his sentences.

Asyndeton, or the lack of connectives, is another Aramaic trait in his style. Anybody who has done Greek composition knows how important it is to connect up one sentence with another by means of suitable linkwords. Where they are lacking, as they so often are in John, we may suspect Aramaic influence.

Other probable Aramaisms are to be found in his odd uses of *hina* and *hoti* possibly concealing an Aramaic *d*[e]; in his employment of the redundant pronoun after a relative (e.g. John 1.27); and in the many examples of *casus pedens*.

But the search for Aramaic influence becomes really fascinating when we not only find many traces of the various kinds of parallelism (synonymous, antithetic, etc.) so characteristic of Hebrew poetry and of Jesus' teaching in the Synoptics, like—

He who comes to me shall never hunger,
And he who believes in me shall never thirst (John 6.35)

or

The thief comes only to steal and kill and destroy:
I came that they may have life, and have it abundantly (John 10.10)

but also evidence (as Dr Matthew Black believes[1]) of Aramaic poetry revealing both strophic arrangement and assonance:

[1] *An Aramaic Approach to the Gospels and Acts*, 109.

He that hath the bride (*kalletha*) is the bridegroom;
He that standeth and heareth him is the friend of the bridegroom
And rejoiceth greatly because of the voice (*qala*) of the bridegroom.
He must increase,
But I must decrease (*qelal*)
This my joy therefore is fulfilled (*kelal*) (John 3.29 f.).

Let these examples suffice. Significantly, most of the Aramaisms occur in the sayings of Jesus rather than in the narrative. What conclusion may we therefore draw? Not that St John translated some Aramaic document word for word (as Torrey said), but certainly that St John was accustomed to think and speak in Aramaic as well as in Greek and probably that in the case of Jesus' sayings he used some kind of logia source—a Johannine Q!

II

Let us pass now to his topography. If this turns out to be as unreliable as has sometimes been asserted, the link we have apparently begun to forge with Palestine will be gravely weakened. The question then is: How does St John's topography look in the light of the latest archaeological researches? Does it consist, for example, with the theory that either he himself, or one of his informants, knew Palestine well? The answer is that it most certainly does.

There are in the Gospel some ten place-names not mentioned in the Synoptic Gospels. Three of these raise no difficulty at all: 'Cana of Galilee', the Pool of Siloam, and the wadi Kidron. Three others give a little more trouble: 'Bethany beyond Jordan', Solomon's Porch, and Ephraim.

If we cannot locate 'Bethany beyond Jordan' precisely, this is not surprising; in the nature of the case a place used for baptizing would be hard to locate later. But that the scene of John's baptizing was in fact beyond Jordan seems to have been established by T. W. Manson.[1]

Nor need we have any serious doubts concerning the precise location of Solomon's Porch. The information which Josephus supplies makes it fairly certain that it formed part of the eastern side of the Court of the Gentiles. Cf. Acts 3.11 and 5.12.

As for Ephraim, there seems to be a general agreement nowadays that it is to be identified with the modern Et-Taiyibeh.

But what of the four remaining place-names: Aenon near Salim, Bethesda, Sychar, and Gabbatha?

---

[1] *The Servant Messiah*, 40.

According to John 3.23 f. Jesus and his disciples came into Judea and baptized, for 'John also was baptizing at Aenon near Salim, because there were many waters there'. The location of Aenon may now be regarded as reasonably certain. East of Gerizim and south-east from Nablus and Shechem lies the town of Salim of which traces survive in Israelite, Hellenistic, and Samaritan literature. And near to Salim lies *Ainun* with a name undoubtedly derived from the Aramaic *Ainon* meaning 'little fountain'. Since these two places lie near the head-waters of Wadi Far'ah, with numerous springs in the neighbourhood, St John might well declare that 'there were many waters there'.

The next place with a question mark over it till recently was the Pool of Bethesda (John 5.2). The pool had never been located and, to make matters worse, the MSS here give a choice of names: Bethzatha, Belzetha, and Bethsaida, besides Bethesda. But now a very strong case for the originality of the reading Bethesda, as well as for the identification of the Pool, has been made out by Jeremias.[1] He tells us how in 1931-2 he watched some excavations beneath a pile of rubbish, a hundred yards north of the Temple, which laid bare, beyond all reasonable doubt, the lost pool of Bethesda, covering an area of some five thousand yards. Quite recently, the Copper Scroll from Qumran has provided confirmation of this.

An old puzzle for scholars was the precise locality of Sychar, with Jacob's well near by (John 4.4 f.). Most of them, for lack of a better alternative, plumped for the modern *Askar* (in Arabic 'military camp'). But *Askar* was not free from objections (as, for instance, Why should the Samaritan woman have come half a mile from *Askar* for water when she might have got it at the *Ain* in her own village?).

E. Sellin's excavations in the area now seem to have provided the true solution. Shechem (Sellin has shown) was not on the site of modern Nablus but at Balatah less than a third as far as Askar from Jacob's well. Balatah was evidently occupied till AD 67 when Vespasian destroyed it with the Temple of Gerizim. The conclusion is that the 'Sychar' of most MSS is a mistake. Here we should follow the Old Syriac Gospels and read 'Sychem', i.e., Shechem.

Where did Pilate judge Jesus? According to John 19.13, he took his seat at a place called the Pavement (*Lithostrōton*) and in Aramaic, Gabbatha. This Pavement was in the Praetorium. But where was it? For decades many have located it at Herod's Palace near the Jaffa Gate. But in the thirties of this century Father L. H. Vincent's researches

[1] *Die Wiederentdeckung von Bethesda* (1949).

seem to have settled the matter in favour of the Antonia Tower, at the north-west corner of the Temple area.[1] There investigation disclosed a pavement covering two thousand five hundred square metres and standing on a rocky elevation to which the name Gabbetha, 'ridge' was fitly applied.

Thus archaeological discovery has, at point after point, confirmed St John's topographical accuracy. Nor is this all. Most of the place-names which occur only in the Fourth Gospel belong to southern Palestine; while Galilean place-names common in the Synoptics, like Nain, Chorazin, Caesarea Philippi and Decapolis, are not found. It looks as if the Fourth Evangelist's traditions about Jesus were specially associated with southern Palestine.

III

We now turn to consider the new light shed by the Dead Sea Scrolls on the Fourth Gospel.

After the alarms and excursions which followed the initial discovery of the Scrolls, we are beginning to appraise their value more realistically; and such experts as Millar Burrows and H. H. Rowley have recently set it on record that, after long study of the Qumran documents, they do not find their understanding of the New Testament substantially affected by them. If there is a possible exception to this, it concerns the conceptual background of the Fourth Gospel. To put the matter in one sentence, the Scrolls have established its essential Jewishness. Down at Khirbet Qumran, on the north-western shore of the Dead Sea and only a few hours' journey from the Judean scenes of the Lord's ministry, lived Jews who thought and spoke in the idioms and antitheses we have been in the habit of calling 'Johannine'.

Anyone who cares to peruse the text of the *Manual of Discipline* can prove this for himself. He will not have gone far before he lights on the very un-Greek phrase 'to do the truth' (cf. John 3.21; I John 1.6) or a reference to 'the sons of light' (John 12.36). A little later, finding an allusion to him who 'looks at the light of life', he will recall Christ's promise of the same 'light of life' to the man who follows him (John 8.12). Further on the *Manual's* words about creation—

By his knowledge everything has been brought into being,
And everything that is, he established by his purpose,
And apart from him, nothing is done

[1] 'L'Antonia et le Prétoire', in *Revue Biblique*, 42 (1933), 83-113.

will ring a Johannine bell in his memory—

> All things were made through him,
> And without him was not any thing made that was made.

In a passage which describes the two spirits—'the spirit of truth' (cf. John 14.17, etc.) and 'the spirit of error' (cf. I John 4.6)—which dominates men's lives, he will learn that 'the sons of error walk in the ways of darkness' and recall Christ's warning against 'walking in darkness' (John 12.35). Finally, this Qumran contrast between the wise man and the foolish—

> According to each man's inheritance in truth he does right, and so he hates error; but according to his possession in the lot of error he does wickedly in it, and so he abhors the truth

will send his mind back to the third chapter of the Fourth Gospel—

> For every one who does evil hates the light, and does not come to the light, lest his deeds should be exposed. But he who does what is true comes to the light that it may be clearly seen that his deeds have been wrought in God (John 3.20 f.).

These comparisons, which could easily be multiplied, strongly suggest that, if we are seeking parallels to the thought-world of St John, we have no need to go ransacking the literature of the Gnostic sects who flourished in the Hellenistic world of the second century. The closest parallels to the antithesis of the Fourth Gospel—light and darkness, truth and error, spirit and flesh—are to be found in the Qumran documents.

This brings us to the cardinal point, on which scholars like K. G. Kuhn, W. F. Albright, Millar Burrows, W. H. Brownlee, Bo Reicke, and J. Jeremias speak with one voice: the dualism which pervades the Johannine writings is of precisely the same kind as we discover in the Dead Sea Scrolls: not physical or substantial (as in the Greek Gnostics) but monotheistic, ethical, and eschatological.

To say that the dualism is monotheistic is another way of saying that it is a modified, not a thorough-going, dualism. The opposition between light and darkness consists not of two eternal and equipollent powers but of two created powers both of which are ultimately subservient to God.

Next, the dualism is ethical. Just as 'light is for him [St John] primarily the symbol of sheer goodness, darkness of moral evil',[1] so it is for the men of Qumran.

---

[1] C. H. Dodd, *The Johannine Epistles*, 18.

Lastly, it is eschatological. Both the men of the Scrolls, and St John see history as the scene of a great battlefield in which light struggles with darkness for the mastery. But if the Qumran sectaries see the *Eschaton* lying in the near future, St John declares that the End has already begun.

It may be useful to compare and contrast the theologies of the Scrolls and St John on four points of detail.[1]

First. Both St John and the sectaries believe (see the words about creation already quoted) in the creation of all by God.

Second. Both see men as ranged in the two opposing 'camps' of light and darkness, each with a personal leader. But, whereas for the sectaries the leader of the sons of light is an angel, i.e. a created being, for St John he is the uncreated Word himself.

Third. Both believe 'there is a war on'. But, whereas for the men of Qumran it is a ding-dong struggle not to be decided till the last great battle—a kind of Armageddon—between the sons of light and the sons of darkness, for St John, the victory is already, in large measure, won— 'the darkness is passing away and the true light is already shining' (I John 2.8).

Fourth. Both St John and the Scrolls agree that the answer to the question, 'What must I do to be saved?' is, 'You must become a son of light'. But, whereas the Qumran view is that this means obedience to the Law, *as interpreted in the Qumran Community*, for St John it means the acceptance of Christ as 'the light of the world' (John 8.12; 12.36, 46).

In fine, the basic difference between the Scrolls and the Fourth Gospel is, as we might have expected, the Fact of Christ.

It has been worthwhile, even shortly, to dwell on the theological differences between the Fourth Gospel and the Scrolls; nevertheless, it is their conceptual resemblances, as they are focused in the doctrines of dualism, which matter most for our present purpose. The conclusion to be drawn is that, if we are searching for parallels to St John's words and ideas, we need not travel further than the caves of Qumran. 'The Scrolls show', says Millar Burrows,[2] 'that we do not need to look outside Palestinian Judaism for the soil in which the Johannine theology grew.' And J. Jeremias,[3] summing up similarly, makes the point, too often forgotten, that the theologies of both the New Testament and of the Scrolls have a common root in the Old Testament. 'Thus the Fourth Gospel is not to be interpreted against the background of Gnostic pre-

---

[1] Here I am indebted to Raymond E. Brown's essay in *The Scrolls and the New Testament* (ed. K. Stendahl), 183-207.
[2] *The Dead Sea Scrolls*, 339 f.
[3] *Exp. Times* 70 (December 1958), 69.

suppositions but against that of Palestinian, Old Testament theological thinking, and of a piety rooted and grounded in the Bible.'

What bearing have these strong resemblances of word and idea between the Scrolls and St John on the question of the Gospel's date and authorship?

They do not, of course, prove the traditional theory of apostolic authorship. But, when taken along with the Evangelist's Aramaicized Greek and his accurate topography of southern Palestine, they make conservative answers much more plausible. On the matter of date we may say this now. Once we realize that the peculiar phraseology of the Gospel is Palestinian, and even pre-Christian, we cannot use it, as scholars once did, as an argument for dating the Gospel late.

To both these questions we shall return. Meanwhile, let us consider next the worth of the historical traditions about Jesus embedded in the Gospel.

IV

That the Fourth Evangelist was not so much a historian intent on setting down the precise order of events as a prophet seeking to declare the ultimate truth of history is a verdict which would command fairly general assent. To be sure, the Synoptics, which are commonly regarded as the better historical sources, are not innocent of theological interpretation. Yet difference there is between the Fourth Gospel and the first three, a difference which may be roughly expressed thus: whereas the Synoptists set the theology in a historical framework, St John sets the history in a theological one—as witness his Prologue which is meant to help the reader to understand the doctrines of his book.

But this does not mean that St John had no interest in history. For one whose dominant conviction found expression in the formula *Logos sarx egeneto* it was surely very important that what he narrates should really have happened. Does then a real core of history underlie his Gospel?

Here inevitably we encounter the question: Did St John know and use the Synoptists' work? Since Streeter discussed the question in his *Four Gospels* (1924), the view that the New Testament writings form a documentary series, in literary dependence on one another, has been losing favour; and Gardner-Smith's *St John and the Synoptic Gospels* (1938) showed how tenuous were the arguments on which Streeter and others relied to prove the dependence of John on Mark and Luke. All we may safely say now is that St John was generally familiar with the oral tradition which was worked into shape in the Synoptics, but that he went his own masterful way in writing his Gospel. For it is abundantly clear that he had access to traditions about Jesus not known to the first three evangelists. What is the historical value of these special traditions of his?

In a problem like this it is hard to lay down criteria for establishing historical value; but one test at least may be suggested. Where something recorded only in the Fourth Gospel helps to make obvious sense of the story of Jesus as we know it from the Synoptics, we may feel tolerably sure that that something is authentic.

With these prolegomena, we may now set down half-a-dozen examples of the worth of St John's historical tradition. It is to St John we owe the information—

(1) that two of Jesus' disciples had formerly followed John the Baptist;
(2) that there was a Judean ministry before the Galilean one;
(3) that at the Feeding of the Five Thousand Messianic excitement reached a dangerous pitch;
(4) that there was a later ministry in the south before the Passion;
(5) that the Last Supper took place before 15th Nisan;
(6) that Jesus appeared before Annas after his arrest.

Let us amplify each of these assertions and defend them.

(1) John 1.35-37 tells how two of the Baptist's disciples decided to follow Jesus after the Baptist had given some strong hint that he believed Jesus to be the Messiah.

Now that some of Jesus' disciples had previously followed the Baptist is historically probable. All Christian accounts of Jesus' ministry begin with the Baptist's mission. The baptism of Jesus might account for this; but it becomes easier to understand if in fact several of Jesus' disciples had previously numbered themselves among the Baptist's followers. And their readiness to follow Jesus becomes more natural if John the Baptist had encouraged them to believe that Jesus was 'the coming One'.

This raises another interesting point. According to the Fourth Gospel, the Baptist recognized Jesus as the Messiah almost from the beginning[1]; whereas the Synoptics (Luke 7.18-23; Matt. 11.2-6, Q) represent him,

---

[1] What did the Baptist mean when he described Jesus as 'the lamb of God which taketh away the sin of the world'? C. H. Dodd takes the title to mean 'the Messiah who makes an end of sin'. Whether we accept this explanation or not, Andrew's claim 'We have found the Messiah' suggests the thoughts that were running in the Baptist's mind.

when imprisoned at Machaerus, sending messengers to ask Jesus if he was indeed he that should come. Is there not here a fatal contradiction between the Fourth Gospel and the Synoptics? On the contrary, may not the two testimonies, between them, preserve the actual truth? With so much Messianic excitement in the air, is it so unlikely that the Baptist and others at first supposed that in Jesus they 'had found the Messiah', but when, with the passage of time and the unfolding of the Galilean ministry, Jesus did not measure up to their ideas of what the Messiah should be and do, their original high hope turned into serious doubt? On such a view, the Baptist's question from prison is completely intel-ligible—and so is Jesus' reply which, after pointing to his healing miracles as the fulfilment of the ancient prophecies, goes on: 'And blessed is he who shall not be offended[1] [put off] in me.' 'I am the Messiah', says the Lord in effect, 'but not the kind of Messiah that you, John, and your friends expected.'

(2) Eusebius[2] preserves a tradition that St John wrote in order to record an early period in Christ's ministry not mentioned by the other evangelists. Was there then a ministry in the south before the Galilean ministry?

Consider St John's record. Some time after his baptism and at 'Bethany beyond Jordan' Jesus met two of the Baptist's disciples whom he added, along with others, to his disciple-band (1.29-51). Later, after briefly visiting Galilee (2.1-12), he returned south and went up to Jerusalem at Passover time: there he cleansed the Temple, won many followers and talked with Nicodemus (2.13-3.21), before exercising for a time a ministry in Judea parallel to John's (3.22-30).

This date for the Temple cleansing is of course a difficulty. Whether the Temple was cleansed thus early, may be doubted; but is there any cogent reason for doubting an early ministry in the south? Besides St John's testimony, we have not only the Synoptic hints that Jesus had visited Jerusalem before his last journey there, but also the implication of Mark 1.14: 'Now after John had been committed to prison Jesus came *into Galilee*' (cf. Matt. 4.12, 'Jesus *withdrew* into Galilee'). Have we not here the reason why Jesus chose Galilee? He had already done enough in the south to run the risk of suffering the same fate as the Baptist.

The whole question was fully and convincingly discussed years ago

---

[1] To be 'offended' (*skandalizesthai*) means to be 'put off' rather than to be 'shocked'. See R. A. Knox, *On Englishing the Bible*.
[2] *Hist. Eccl.* III, 27.

by Scott Holland.[1] He sums up: 'On every ground, by virtue of all the converging evidences, there had been a ministry in Jerusalem; and the Synoptic Gospels make it certain that this ministry had been attempted before the mission in Galilee had begun. Now it is the Fourth Gospel which alone tells us what this Ministry was, and when it happened.'

(3) We turn now to the Feeding of the Five Thousand which was the climax of the Galilean Ministry.

St Mark relates that when the feeding was over, Jesus 'at once *compelled* his disciples to embark on the boat and proceed towards Bethany, while he himself was dismissing the crowd'.

Why did Jesus have to do this? John 6.15 gives the answer: 'Perceiving that they were about to come and kidnap him in order to make him King [i.e. King of Israel, Messiah: cf. John 1.29], Jesus withdrew again to the hills by himself.'

Here surely is 'the moment of truth'. Once we understand John's comment, the temperature of the whole story suddenly rises, and we begin to realize what was happening. None has taken the point better than T. W. Manson.[2] He points out that 'sheep without a shepherd' means not a congregation without a minister but a nation without a national leader. He notes that Mark speaks of five thousand *men*, as distinct from women and children. Then he goes on: 'What Jesus saw on the shore of the lake was a Maccabaean host with no Judas Maccabaeus, a leaderless mob, a danger to themselves and to everyone else.' This is why Jesus first compelled the disciples to depart, and then stayed behind to disperse the crowd. It looks as if the sympathies of the disciples were with the crowd rather than with the purposes of Jesus. Now it is a single verse in St John which supplies the decisive clue here. Surely this is history, if anything in the Gospel records is.

(4) As St John testifies to a preliminary Judean ministry, so in chs. 7-11 he testifies to a later one in the south. Can we accept his testimony?

Many passages in John 7-11 suggest that the Evangelist had access to reliable historical information about the last few months of Jesus' ministry. Let the reader re-read 7.10-15, 25-27, 31-32, 37, 40-52; 8.20; 10.22-24, 40-42; 11.54-59, and unless he has a hopeless bias against the historical value of the Gospel, he will be compelled to admit that a great deal here is extraordinarily vivid and has the ring of truth. Now, among these veridical passages, we find six notes about Jesus' movements:

---

[1] *The Fourth Gospel*, 361.   [2] *The Servant Messiah*, 70 f.

7.10—Jesus went up to Jerusalem at the Feast of Tabernacles.

10.22—Jesus was teaching in Solomon's porch at the Feast of Dedication, the weather being wintry.

10.40—Jesus retired to Transjordan.

11.17—Jesus travelled from Transjordan to Bethany.

11.54—Because of growing hostility, Jesus retired with his disciples to Ephraim, near the wilderness.

12.1——Six days before the Passover he came to Bethany and, the day after, entered Jerusalem.

On the basis of this evidence Goguel,[1] who believes the Johannine historical tradition here to be reliable, suggests the following account of Jesus' movements during the last part of his ministry:

(a) Jesus left Galilee and went up to the Feast of Tabernacles (end of September)—John 7.10.

(b) There he taught for three months until the Feast of Dedication (last week of December)—John 10.22.

(c) Soon after, because of mounting hostility, Jesus retired to Transjordan (Perea)—John 10.40.

(d) Six days before the Passover (i.e. the beginning of April) he returned to Jerusalem—John 12.1.

Goguel's view has commended itself to a number of good scholars.[2] If he is right, the Fourth Gospel implies a period of six months, including a three months' ministry in Jerusalem, between Jesus' departure from Galilee and the final Passover.

Can this be reconciled with Mark's record? *Prima facie*, the answer looks to be 'No'. After Jesus leaves Galilee, so swiftly does Mark's narrative move that we readily imagine events followed hot-foot on each other and compress the happenings of Mark 10.46-16.8 into a single week. Did things really happen so? In an important article[3] T. W. Manson has shown that, if we examine Mark's narrative carefully, we shall find that the events related in Mark 10-16 occupied at least *six months*. Note, in particular, the implications of Mark 10.1: 'He came into the territories of Judea and Transjordan, and there came to him crowds and again he taught them.'

If we have regarded this as a trip from Galilee to the south with a little teaching by the way, we had better think again. It is the record of a *ministry* in Judea (and presumably in Jerusalem) and Perea, with different groups of people in these districts receiving instruction from the

---

[1] *The Life of Jesus*, 238-50, 401-28.
[2] V. Taylor, J. E. Davey, etc.
[3] *Bulletin of the John Rylands Lib.* 33 (1950-1), 271-82.

Lord. Thus the time involved (six months) and the territory visited (Judea and Perea) are roughly the same as in John's record.

One more word. It has long been felt that the various Jerusalem controversies between Jesus and the authorities, recorded in Mark 11 and 12, may not have fallen out exactly as they stand now in Mark, i.e. need not all be located in Passion Week. It may now be suggested that some in fact occurred during the three months' ministry in Jerusalem which preceded Jesus retirement to Transjordan. Three examples may be cited:

    (a) The challenge to Jesus' authority (Mark 11.27 ff.; John 7.14 ff.).

    (b) The Messiah's Davidic Sonship (Mark 12.35-37; John 7.40-44).

    (c) Jesus in the Treasury (Mark 12.41; John 8.20).

    (5) St John is clear that the Last Supper took place before Nisan 15 (John 13.1; 18.28). Is he right on this point also?

In his *Eucharistic Words of Jesus* (1955) J. Jeremias argued impressively that the Last Supper was a Passover and took place on 15th Nisan, which began at sunset. If Jeremias is right about the date, St John is wrong. But is he? Not a few scholars, while willing to believe that the Last Supper was some sort of Passover (perhaps an anticipated one), are not persuaded that he is. Can we take the matter any further? Following T. W. Manson's lead, Dr M. Black[1] has recently produced quite convincing evidence that Mark's record of events from the Last Supper to the Crucifixion is also 'telescoped'. As it stands, you get the impression that everything was over in a single night and morning—the Supper, the Arrest, the two Trials, one Jewish and one Roman. On the face of it this seems incredible; and by appeal to Luke's special Passion-source (a hypothesis accepted by many), Black persuasively suggests that one or even two full days intervened between the Supper and the Crucifixion. Following Mlle Jaubert, he cites patristic evidence and the calendrical evidence of the Dead Sea Scrolls to show that the Passover of Crucifixion year cannot have been observed by all Jews on 15th Nisan; since the Qumran sectaries, and possibly the Sadducees, following the old priestly calendar, may have kept Passover earlier than 15th Nisan. And whatever we may have thought about it before, St John's Last Supper has at least four definitely paschal features. (The meal was *at night*; the disciples *reclined* at it; a *sop* was given; and there was a suggestion about 'giving something to the poor'.)

Perhaps therefore we should seek a solution to this most complicated of all New Testament problems in the view that the Last Supper was in

[1] *New Testament Essays* (in memory of T. W. Manson), 19-33.

fact an *irregular Passover* celebrated a day or two before the date laid
down by the Pharisees. If this is so, must we not admit that on a further
point of history St John may well be right?

(6) Finally, it is probable that in his account of the Trial of Jesus
St John has preserved at least two good historical traditions.

One of the difficulties in Mark's account is his statement that the
Sanhedrin met at night to try Jesus. Since nocturnal meetings of the
Council were illegal, many scholars believe Luke is right in relating a
formal meeting of the Sanhedrin at day-break. But may there not well
have been also an *informal* hearing at night? St John says there was a
hearing, and that Annas, the ex-high-priest (and still 'the power behind
the throne') presided over it (John 18.12-14, 19-24). There is no reason
why this should not be good history, as even Klausner admits.

Our final point has already been mentioned; Pilate's Pretorium, where
he tried Jesus, was in the Tower Antonia, as L. H. Vincent's researches
have shown.

Enough has been said to show how much good history lies behind the
Fourth Gospel. Once again, the question poses itself: How did the
Fourth Evangelist come by it, if he was writing in far-away Ephesus and,
say, fifty years after the event? Who was the Fourth Evangelist?

V

In our epilogue we can only glance at this question. But this much
may be said. The trend of recent studies has been to make the Evangelist's links with Palestine much stronger than many of us have allowed.
Here is a man whose Greek conceals an Aramaic mother-tongue, who
writes as if he had known Jerusalem and its environs well, whose cast of
mind—witness the Dead Sea Scrolls—is Palestinian, and who obviously
had access to some excellent historical traditions about Jesus. Yet his
book was written in Ephesus.

If anyone is minded to explain, say, the accurate topography by the
theory that this Christian from Ephesus had visited the Holy Land in
order to identify the sacred sites, he is guilty of anachronism. The destruction of Jerusalem between 66 and 70 makes it reasonably certain
that whoever supplied the topography—not to mention the tradition of
Jesus' words and works—must have known Jerusalem and its neighbourhood before AD 65.

Could it have been the Apostle John himself? (We agree with W. L.
Knox that those who accept the early martyrdom of the Apostle show a
quite monumental preference for the inferior evidence.) We cannot dis-

prove it; yet many of the old objections to such a view (the silence of Ignatius, the comparative 'unknownness' of the Gospel in the second century, its contrasts with the Synoptic record, etc.) give us pause. What we may hold *contra mundum* is that the Beloved Disciple was the Apostle John, and that his testimony stands behind the Gospel. But if not the Apostle, why not a close disciple of the Apostle, himself a Palestinian Jew, who, having known the Holy Land in the first half of the century, later made his way to Ephesus? That this man was also the Presbyter of the Johannine Epistles seems also (*pace* C. H. Dodd) reasonably certain. Need we say more—unless we go on to say that the Presbyter must have been Papias's Presbyter John? In that case the Gospel is the Gospel of John the Elder according to John the Apostle.

We call it the Fourth Gospel. But is it literally and chronologically so? We can no longer make John's peculiar phraseology an argument for a late date. The Rylands Fragment has persuaded even Bultmann that a date later than 100 is unlikely. The growing opinion that St John did not know the Synoptic Gospels means that we need not date the Fourth Gospel, say, ten or fifteen years after them. It might have been written about 80; but then again it might have been written a decade earlier.

VII

THE STYLE OF ST PAUL

Is there any writer of whom Buffon's 'The style is the man' is truer than St Paul? For the apostle letter-writing was a substitute for personal action; and when he took his pen in his hand—or dictated to his amanuensis—the whole man—all his energy, passion, pride, sympathy and tenderness—went down on the papyrus.

Paul's Greek is not literary or bookish. It does not smell of the lamp. He did not choose his words to please the purists or construct his sentences with the sedulous care of a Plato or a Pater. Yet if his Greek is non-literary, it is leagues away from the artless and ungrammatical vernacular of the papyri. The reason is simple: if Paul was not a university graduate, he was a man of excellent education, an education that owed much to both Judaism and Hellenism. So we get the paradox that, though Paul is, in Gilbert Murray's phrase, 'one of the great figures of Greek literature', a notable classical scholar like Norden can confess: 'Paul is a writer whom I at least only understand with great difficulty.' This bewildering element in Paul's Greek is due to its Semitic undertone, to the fact that his Greek words (e.g. *dikaiosynē*) carry Hebraic nuances. (And, so very often, *la vérité consiste dans les nuances.*) In fine, his writing is as full of subconscious recollections of the Greek Old Testament as *The Pilgrim's Progress* is full of echoes of the King James Bible.

Was Paul trained as a rhetorician, and does he employ any of the arts of the self-conscious stylist? If we may trust his own testimony, the answer must be No. He was ready to concede that he was 'rude in speech' (II Cor. 11.6), as he disclaimed all skill in rhetoric: 'My speech and my message were not in plausible words of wisdom but in demonstration of the Spirit and of power' (I Cor. 2.4). Yet we must take Paul's estimate of his own oratorical expertise with a grain of salt, if only for the very good reason that, judged by results, he was a mightily effective speaker. This is surely the final test.

Yet though Paul disdained the tricks and tropes of the rhetorician, his letters contain more art than appears at first sight. One might pick out half a dozen passages which reveal high artistic skill, and were hardly composed on the spur of the moment, or *currente calamo*. We may pass over Phil. 2.6-11 because it is now widely held to be a pre-Pauline Christian hymn. But notice the careful construction of Rom. 14.7 ff.:

None of us lives to himself and none of us dies to himself.
If we live, we live to the Lord, and if we die, we die to the Lord;
So then, whether we live or whether we die, we are the Lord's.
For to this end Christ died and lived again,
That he might be Lord both of the dead and of the living.

Such symmetrical parallelism, with its rhythm and cadence, shows as much artistry as a lyric of Burns. But beyond question the finest example is Paul's 'Song of Songs' in 1 Corinthians 13. We print it usually as prose, but it is certainly poetry and ought always to be printed as in Moffatt's translation:

I may speak with the tongues of men and of angels,
    but if I have no love,
        I am a noisy gong or a clanging cymbal;
I may prophesy, fathom all mysteries and secret lore,
I may have such absolute faith that I can move hills from their place,
    but if I have no love,
        I count for nothing.
I may distribute all I possess in charity
I may give up my body to be burnt,
    but if I have no love,
        I make nothing of it.

Notice the choice of words, the figures of speech, the rhythm and design. This artistry, surely not unconscious, plus the fact that the passage fits very loosely into the context, which is a discussion of 'spiritual gifts', strongly suggest that the apostle did not improvise it in 'the flowering instant'. Johannes Weiss was probably right when he called it a deliberate 'creation'—created like a poem of Goethe.

Now let us try to characterize Paul as a writer in more detail. But, to begin with, let us contrast him with St John. The Roman Catholic theologian Mersch has done it superbly:

Paul was converted in the way that best suits the character of Paul. The Word of God leaped forth on him like a robber, and in consequence there remained an element of aggressiveness and abruptness even in his style. John was of a different stamp, and God won him as befitted John. The truth unveiled itself within his soul, as a summer landscape rises before one's eyes at eventide.

The 'abruptness' to which Mersch refers finds illustration in Paul's fondness for antithesis. Pointed contrasts appeal to the Apostle. Training may have something to do with this, but surely its ultimate source lies in Paul's temperament—he had one of these 'either-or' natures— and in his experience—his conversion had cut his life in two. At any rate he was a master of antithesis. Rom. 6.23 yields a splendid short example:

Sin's wage is death, but God's gift is life eternal in Christ Jesus our Lord.

For a longer but no less memorable one we may turn to I Cor. 15.42 f where Paul is discussing 'the spiritual body':

> What is sown is mortal,
> What rises is immortal.
> Sown inglorious,
> It rises in glory;
> Sown in weakness,
> It rises in power;
> Sown an animate body,
> It rises a spiritual body.

Consider, next, Paul's use of the Diatribe style in argument. This was the dialectical manner which Cynic and Stoic itinerant preachers had popularized in their street-corner sermons; and no doubt Paul had often heard them at it. The essence of it is apostrophe and question-cum-answer. You conjure up an imaginary opponent—in Romans 2 and 3 it is 'the Jewish objector'—and you argue the case with him. He raises an objection or difficulty ('Then what advantage has the Jew?' Rom. 3.1) and in your reply you demolish it—and him. For an example, take I Cor. 15.35 f. 'But someone will ask, How are the dead raised? Thou fool . . . that which thou sowest is not quickened, except it die.' Often, however, Paul's rejoinder is a brief but expressive *mē genoito* ! 'Does that mean that Christ is an abettor of sin? No, never!' (Gal. 2.17).

A third feature of Paul's style is his love of metaphor. In this he is a true Oriental, delighting in picture-language, and drawing his figures from every aspect of life.

Agriculture gives him: 'I planted, Apollus watered, but God gave the growth' (I Cor. 3.6) as, a few verses later, architecture supplies him with: 'Like a skilled master-builder I laid a foundation.' Military metaphors abound: 'If the bugle gives an indistinct sound, who will get ready for battle?' (I Cor. 14.8); 'Put on the whole armour of God' (Eph.

5.11); 'the weapons of our warfare are not worldly' (II Cor. 10.4); 'the peace of God ... will garrison your hearts' (Phil. 4.7). So do athletic figures, with the stadium and the arena forming the background: 'Run to win' (I Cor. 9.24); 'I do not box as one beating the air' (I Cor. 9.26); 'I press on toward the goal for the prize' (Phil. 3.14); 'I have fought with wild beasts at Ephesus' (I Cor. 15.32); 'we wrestle not with flesh and blood' (Eph. 6.12). Inevitably Paul the Roman citizen raids politics for some of his images: 'Our capital city (*politeuma*) is in heaven' (Phil. 3.20); 'you are no longer strangers and sojourners but you are fellow citizens with the saints' (Eph. 2.19); 'so then we are ambassadors for Christ' (II Cor. 5.20). The world of commerce supplies its quota: the apostles are not 'pedlars of God's word' (II Cor. 2.17); the Holy Spirit in our hearts is 'the first instalment' (*arrabōn*) of our heavenly inheritance (II Cor. 1.22); and Paul tells the Philippians that he 'seeks the interest that accrues to their credit' (Phil. 4.17).

When you remember that every second man on the streets of Ephesus or Corinth was a slave, it is not surprising to find Paul describing sin as slavery or salvation as 'emancipation' in terms which (as Deissmann has shown) can be closely paralleled from contemporary papyri. Household images are likewise common: the apostles are 'stewards of the mysteries of God' (I Cor. 4.1); Christians are adopted sons of God (Gal. 4.5, etc.); and the law has proved our *paidagōgos* (nurse, chaperon and tutor all in one) unto Christ (Gal. 3.24). We find also, naturally enough, sacrificial and sacerdotal figures like *thusia*, *hilastērion* and *leitourgos*. But far more important are Paul's legal metaphors, especially that of justification'. He pictures salvation as a court-room acquittal, and, by a tremendous paradox, calls God a judge who acquits guilty men (Rom. 3.24; 4.5; 8.1 ff., 30 ff.). But perhaps his most famous figure is anatomical: 'You are the body of Christ' (I Cor. 12.27), a metaphor so influential in Christian thinking down the centuries that one modern theologian has made it the master-key to Paul's whole Gospel.

Faults in plenty Paul has as a writer. He can be as obscure as Browning (see Gal. 2.3-6: to this day we cannot be sure whether Titus was circumcised or not). He can be turgid and hyperbolical. He can commit an occasional solecism—see Phil. 2.1. And he often produces what the grammarians call *anacoloutha* (e.g. Rom. 5.12 f.). But these inconcinnities are mere spots on the sun. They are the faults of a man in great haste on his Lord's business: you do not stop to polish your phrases when your converts are 'resiling' (a good Scots metaphor) from the grace of God (as in Galatia), or 'downing tools' to scan the sky for a returning Christ (as in Thessalonika), or getting drunk at the Holy Communion (as at Corinth).

All in all, Paul shows astonishing versatility. The indignation of Galatians, when he writes with his nerves in 'a kind of blaze', differs *toto caelo* from the affection of Philippians ('O foolish Galatians'—'my brethren whom I love and long for, my joy and crown'). How different is Romans from Philemon! The differences are of course partly due to subject matter and the circumstances which occasioned the letters, but partly also to the man who can 'change his tone' and 'become all things to all men'. All his most characteristic moods are mirrored in his correspondence: anger (Gal. 3.1), grief (Rom. 9.3), pride (II Cor. 11.5), defiance (Gal. 6.17), irony (I Cor. 4.8-10) and, of course, affection (II Cor. 7.2 f.; Phil. 4.1).

Paul's is 'the style of genius if not the genius of style'. His rhetoric is the rhetoric of the heart rather than of the schools. If he rises to great heights (as in the magnificent paradoxes of II Cor. 6.8-10 so wonderfully rendered in the New English Bible) it is not because he has spent painful hours prettifying his periods, but because he is overmastered by the greatness of his theme, and the theme demands noble words. The saying of Longinus that 'sublimity is the echo of a great soul' finds no better illustration than in Paul of Tarsus. Sometimes that soul will utter itself in words of commanding simplicity:

> Whatever is true, whatever is honourable, whatever is just, whatever is pure, whatever is lovely, whatever is gracious, if there is any excellence, if there is anything worthy of praise, think about these things (Phil. 4.8).

At other times it will take wings and soar into the empyrean:

> For I am persuaded that neither death nor life, nor angels nor principalities nor powers, nor things present nor things to come, nor height nor depth, nor anything else in all creation will be able to separate us from the love of God, which is in Christ Jesus our Lord (Rom. 8.38 f.).

Part Two

NEW TESTAMENT PREACHING

VIII

WHAT IS CHRISTIANITY?

'Your faith in Christ Jesus . . . the love which ye have to all the saints . . . the hope which is laid up for you in heaven'—Col. 1.4f.

SUPPOSE you were sitting on a Brains Trust when the question-master put the question, 'What is Christianity?' how would you answer?

It is not a simple question. Is Christianity a creed to be believed? Is it a life to be lived? Or is it a means of getting a passport into heaven?

One man will tell you that what you believe is what really matters. Another will say, 'I don't give a fig for your creeds. The life's the thing.' And another will tell you that the chief thing is to be 'saved', that is, to be sure that you are going to heaven.

Are all these answers quite wrong? Surely not. But surely also none of them is big enough, deep enough, comprehensive enough. But if so, where are we to look for an answer?

When you are faced with a difficult problem in law, or science, or in economics, you don't go to Tom, Dick or Harry for an answer. If you are a wise man, you go to an expert—an expert on the subject. Well, here is a difficult question—so let us go to an expert. And to whom can we better go than to St Paul? By common consent, St Paul was an expert on Christianity. He taught it; he lived it; he died for it. And I suggest that you won't find a better clue to the answer we are seeking than in these three little words to which St Paul keeps coming back again and again in his letters—I mean, faith and hope and love. If we can find out what he meant by these words, we shall be well on the way to an answer.

I

The first thing is 'faith'. Faith is of the essence of Christianity. But what does it mean? Well, though faith is one of those words that can mean a great many things—from blind credulity to barren orthodoxy—there is no doubt what it meant for St Paul. It was 'faith in Christ Jesus'. It was directed not to a proposition but to a person—a living person. It was utter trust in the living Christ, the Christ who had died to redeem

F

men from their sins. St Paul once defined that faith in one of his great sentences. 'The life that I now live in the flesh,' he said, 'I live by faith.' What kind of faith? 'Faith in the Son of God who loved me and gave himself for me.'

How does a man get such a faith? Faith 'comes from hearing', hearing the Gospel. And a man gets such a faith when he responds with all his heart to the Good News of the Grace of God to sinners in the Cross of Jesus Christ. When a sinful man—and we are all sinners—hears the Story of the Cross aright—when as he gazes upon 'that Strange Man' hanging there, he sees not simply one more Jew dying a malefactor's death but the very God himself bearing in his Son the sin of the whole world—when, as he surveys the wondrous Cross, there breaks upon his soul the revelation 'God loved like that!', what is that man to do? If a man, with the sense of his sin upon him, once sees the Cross like that, there is only one thing for him to do—to surrender himself to that sin-bearing love of God which meets him in the Cross, and to do so unconditionally, unreservedly and for ever.

Yes, for ever. For faith is not the act of a moment only, but the attitude of a whole life. It is not merely once to affirm, 'I believe in Christ' but to go on believing in him day after day, year after year, and counting that the highest wisdom God has given you under this visiting moon.

This is Christian faith—in P. T. Forsyth's fine phrase, 'the grand venture in which we commit our whole soul and future to the confidence that Christ is not an illusion but the reality of God'.

And this brings us to the second part of the text.

II

'The love which ye have to all the saints.' Faith and love belong together. You cannot separate them. If faith is one side of the medal, love is the other. 'Faith,' says St Paul, our expert, 'works through love' —finds expression in love, flowers in love—or it is not faith at all but a sham and a husk—'Though I have all faith so that I could remove mountains, and have not love, I am nothing.'

What does St Paul mean by 'love'?

The Greek language he wrote has at least three words for 'love'. First, *eros*. This is the love which craves and, at its lowest, lusts. You will not find it in the New Testament. Then there is *philia*, 'friendship'—mutual affection between kindred spirits like David and Jonathan. You will find it once in the New Testament. The third word is *agapē*; and the New Testament resounds with it from end to end. *Agapē* is the love which seeks not to possess but to give, to spend and to be spent for the object beloved. 'If *eros* is all take, and *philia* is give-and-take, *agapē* is all give.' This is St Paul's word for love.

Is it then some kind of emotion? No, there is nothing sloppy or sentimental about it. True, there may come relations in life where *agapē* is associated with emotion, but *agapē* is something more. This something more can be expressed by no less a word than life. Christian love is a new way of living which came into our world with Christ. It is a new way of living for God and for our fellow-men because God has so loved us in Christ. In some ways, our best English equivalent for it is 'caring'—caring for others because God has cared for us.

For the rest, if you want to know how it expresses itself, you have Paul's 'Song of Songs' in I Corinthians 13 to tell you. There is the thing itself—*agapē* in action—'long suffering and very kind, free from envy and making no parade'—you know the rest—'bearing all things, believing all things, hoping all things, enduring all things'. And this love is the way of life for all who call Christ Saviour. It is the energy we are called on to radiate among our fellow-men. 'By this,' says our Lord, 'shall all men know that you are my disciples if you have love one to another.'

III

The last of the little words is hope: 'the hope which is laid up for you in heaven.'

I cannot help thinking that hope has been the Cinderella in our trinity of Christian graces. Ever since Paul's day preachers have insisted on the importance of faith; and we have always been willing to talk about love, even if we have not always been willing to turn it into deeds and make it real. But hope certainly does not have the place in our thinking today that it occupies in the New Testament. There that radiant little word sings out again and again with the note of a joy bell. We read of 'the God of hope', 'the hope of the Gospel', 'Christ Jesus our hope'. St Peter speaks of the 'living hope' which is ours ever since Christ 'left one gaping tomb in the wide graveyard of the world'. And the Writer to the Hebrews calls hope 'the anchor within the veil'.

This New Testament hope, be it noted, is never a vague, nebulous optimism that somehow in the end things will turn out all right. It is always religious hope—hope which rests not on man but on God, the God and Father of Jesus Christ.

Now turn to the text: 'the hope which is laid up for you in heaven'.

Here the word 'hope' really stands for the object of hope, that is, the heavenly blessedness which God has prepared for those who love him. Now such a hope is, or ought to be, immensely important for our present living. R. L. Stevenson somewhere recalls a conversation he had with a Fife labourer who was 'mucking a byre' (*Anglice* but inadequately: 'cleaning a cowshed'). They talked of many things, and especially of the aims and ends of life. And, as they conversed, one casual but memorable remark revealed the labourer for the man he was. 'Him that has aye something ayont', he said, 'need never be weary.' That man knew by instinct what the New Testament means by hope.

What is the essence of Christianity? Do I go far wrong if I sum it up as faith in God through Jesus Christ, the living Crucified, plus love— *agapē*—to our fellow-men, plus the hope of the life immortal?

The practical questions remain, as they always do. Do we hold that faith—or, rather, does that faith hold us? If it does, then the next question 'Do we walk in love?' answers itself. That kind of faith must work through love. And if we hold that faith and walk in love, we can leave the rest to the God and Father of Christ. For it is the hope of the Gospel that those who 'live by faith in the Son of God', who are united to him by faith as by fetters of adamant, shall one day see him as he is in glory everlasting.

IX

ON THINKING BIGLY

'Tell out, my soul, the greatness of the Lord'
—*Luke 1.46 (New English Bible)*.

'WHAT we need,' said the old Highland minister who never used one word when he could use three, 'is height—elevation—altitude.'

But the old man had something. I wonder if we Christians think bigly enough. It is told of a certain statesman that he once said to his colleagues, gathered to consider some policy of high importance, 'Gentlemen, you must consult bigger maps.' Don't we Christians—especially in these 'man-into-space' days—need to consult bigger spiritual maps?

I

Take, first, our ideas about God. 'Your God is too small,' Mr J. B. Phillips tells us in one of his books. And he's dead right. In what puny and paltry ways we too often think about him! How we scale him down, especially in time of war, to the dimensions of our own country! And the unimaginably great God, the 'Lord of all being, throned afar, Whose glory flames from sun and star' . . . is dwindled down to the stature of a national patron saint. We smile at Jonah in the Bible story—Jonah the man who thought he could run away from God by taking ship to Tarshish, fondly supposing that, once there, he would be where the writ of the Almighty did not run. We smile at Jonah, but how very like him we are ourselves! We think and talk as if the All Highest were the God of our particular denomination, or the Defender of the Protestant Faith, or the Father of the white man only. But the Bible never encourages us to do this. To be sure, the Bible knows nothing of the modern scientist's notion of an expanding universe. But its God is never too small for man to imagine that he can run away from him or get lost in the immensities of his universe. Listen—

> Whither shall I go from thy spirit?
> Or whither shall I flee from thy presence?
> If I ascend up into heaven, thou art there,
> If I make my bed in hell, behold, thou art there.

Or again,

> For I am persuaded that neither death nor life, nor angels, nor principalities, nor powers, nor things present, nor things to come, nor height, nor depth, nor any other created thing shall be able to separate us from the love of God, which is in Christ Jesus our Lord.

'Our God,' we say, and say truly. But he isn't ours only. He is the God of the Russians, though their rulers refuse him worship. And the God of the Japanese, though they make their Emperor in the image of the All Highest. And the God of the Hottentot and the Bantu, the Dyak and the Patagonian, though in their blindness they bow down to wood and stone. The God of all men, whose tender mercies are over all his works; the God who made all worlds and sovereignly shapes the course of history; and who in Christ his only Son has stooped low to bless and redeem us, that you and I might lift up praying hands to the unseen, crying 'Abba, Father'.

This, and nothing less, is the God whom we adore. Don't we need to use bigger spiritual maps? As big as our Moderator Dr Burleigh's, when, in thanking Sir Bernard Lovell for telling the Assembly about the astronomers' immensities, he added: 'But we believe that our God rules over all your worlds.'

II

And as we scale down the great God, don't we tend to take small views of him whom we call his Son?

To our small thinking, the great Head of the Church, who came proclaiming a Kingdom mightier than Caesar's and speaking as never man spake, who knew himself to be the unique Son of the unseen Father as he knew himself destined for the throne of the universe, who gave his life as a ransom for the sins of the world and, after he had risen, promised his abiding Presence to his followers to the end of time—to our small thinking, I say, this immeasurably great Person becomes, at worst, a sort of super Sunday School Teacher and, at best, 'the finest man who ever lived'.

So we domesticate God's lightning from heaven and dwindle down his great accents into pious platitudes and moral commonplaces. And the *real* Christ, the only Christ who explains Christianity, the Christ of the incomparable teaching and the mighty works; the Christ who first hallowed the grave and then left it empty; the Christ whom St Paul calls 'the fulness of the Godhead, bodily' and St John, 'the Word made flesh'; the Christ of Dali's great picture whose Cross is set as a saving symbol in the immensities of the universe—this Christ becomes little more than a gifted Semite of the first century AD.

So we turn the Lord Jesus into a noble figure in an antique story, forgetting that by the shining miracle of the first Easter Day he has become a living and ubiquitous Lord, 'let loose in the world where neither Roman nor Jew can stop his truth'; a Christ who was with St John on the convict isle of Patmos and with Peter in Nero's Rome, with Latimer and Ridley in the fire, with Bunyan in his Bedford gaol and Margaret Wilson in the cruel Solway tide, with Livingstone and Mary Slessor in darkest Africa—aye, and today with Schweitzer in the swamps of Lambarene:

> No dead fact stranded on the shore
> Of the oblivious years:
> But warm, sweet, tender even yet;

a Christ who still travels the world in the greatness of his strength, mighty to save; a Christ who is a perennial Presence to those who love him, the same yesterday, today and for ever.

III

God, Christ—we come, last of all, to *man*, and here too have we not tragically lost dimension?

Once we thought bigly of man, made in the image of God. I think of our forefathers framing the *Shorter Catechism*. 'What is the chief end of man?' they began, and how nobly they answered: 'Man's chief end is to glorify God and enjoy him for ever.' Or I think of the character in George Douglas Brown's *House with the Green Shutters* who said: 'He was a great fellow, my friend Will. The thumb mark of his Maker was wet in the clay of him.' We do not talk this idiom nowadays—it has gone right out of fashion, for today man's chief end seems to be filling up football coupons or idolizing the latest film or television star.

What has caused this diminished, this dehumanized, view of man? Many things, doubtless. The coming of the age of industrial science which tends to see man only as a tiny cog in a great machine. The influence of a materialistic psychology which regards man as a mere bundle of conditioned reflexes, like Pavlov's salivating dogs—that is another cause. Above all, the rising tide of secularism which regards man as wholly a being of this temporal order and robs his life of its eternal dimensions. But, whatever the causes, the fact is undoubted. We do not speak much nowadays of man as a creature made in God's image, as a creature with a foot in *two* worlds: who, if he is, on his one side, of the earth, earthy, is, on the other side, a creature with a Divine destiny, made for fellowship with God and the Life Everlasting.

One great need of our time is just this—to recapture the Christian doctrine of man. No other religion takes such a lofty view of man's dignity. To be sure, Christianity is realistic—it does not blink the facts. It insists that man is a fallen creature: it talks of 'original sin'. But it no less insists that man is a being in whose heart God has set eternity, and that he will never find peace until he realizes it.

'Gentlemen, you must consult bigger maps.' We are summoned to think bigly as Christians: to think bigly of God who is our Maker, of Christ who is our Saviour, and of man, the being for whom God did not spare his only Son, the brother for whom Christ died.

One night, Lord Tennyson and a friend fell to discussing what they sought from life. 'I ask,' said the friend, 'that I should leave the world a better place than I found it.' 'And I,' said the poet, 'that I should have a new vision of God.'

A new vision of God, of Christ, of man—a new and bigger vision—is not this one of the things for which our world is weary and waiting? But such a vision can only become a reality if it begin—if it take shape and grow—in the hearts of individual men and women like you and me. Shall we not say to God, 'Lord, give us this bigger vision—and begin with me'?

'Tell out, my soul, the greatness of the Lord.'

X

THE ACTION SERMONS OF CHRIST

'He took a child'—Mark 9.36.
'He took a towel'—John 13.4.
'He took a loaf'—Mark 14.22.

DID you ever hear the expression 'the Action Sermon'? Our fore-fathers applied it to the sermon preached just before the celebration of the Lord's Supper. In point of fact, of course, the real Action Sermon was the Supper itself; but we'll come to that in a moment.

'Actions,' they say, 'speak louder than words.' A simple action, inno-cent of any speech, will often speak more movingly than a multitude of words. Nay, there come times, situations, experiences when we know what poor and paltry things words can be. 'The highest cannot be spoken,' said Goethe, 'it can only be acted.' Our Lord knew this, and on at least half a dozen occasions chose to speak by deeds rather than by words. Let us take three of them for study.

I

First, 'He took a child.' Not an eagle, not a lion: just a child. He took a child and set him in the midst of the disputing disciples.

Need I remind you of our Lord's peculiar regard for children? How fragrant the Gospels are with tender allusions to the little folk! How he watched them playing marriages and funerals in the market-place! How his indignation blazed out at the disciples for belittling them! How pleased he was with their praises when all others seemed turning against him! Now, this regard for children is really one of the unique things in our Lord. You may search the literature of antiquity from end to end, and you will not find its like. Nevertheless, for Christ, the little child, precious indeed in his own right, was something more. Listen: 'Whoso-ever shall not receive the Kingdom of God as a little child, he shall not enter therein.' For Christ, the child was a living symbol of the character needed for God's Kingdom.

Was it then the *innocence* of the child that Christ was calling for? No, this is where many of us go wrong. Jesus came to save sinners, not

innocents. Moreover, whatever doting parents may say, little children
are *not* always little innocents—ask any nursemaid! No, it is the relationship of the child which Christ has in mind. A child depends entirely
on its parents. Everything comes from them—is their gift. The child's
part is to receive, not to earn. Not the innocence but the receptiveness
of the child is what Christ is calling for. Unless we are ready to receive
God's Kingdom—his salvation—as a child takes a present from his
father's hand—we shall not have it.

'Whosoever shall not receive the Kingdom of God as a little child . . .'
It is still true. Men still enter God's Kingdom in the same way. The
Kingdom of our Father is not for the proud and self-sufficient—the
men who imagine that they are righteous and can save themselves. The
Kingdom still belongs to the humble-of-heart—to the men and women
who, owning their weakness and confessing their sinfulness, cast them-
selves on God's mercy and forgiveness freely offered to them in the
Cross of Christ.

II

'He took a towel.'

You remember the scene of this acted parable. It was the Upper
Room, the night before the Crucifixion. The Supper had begun, that
Supper to which all our Lord's Suppers run back—when suddenly
(Luke says) contention flared up among the Twelve. Think of it—Jesus
their master presently going out to the Agony and the Cross, and these
disciples are still quarrelling about who is to be greatest—still blinded
by visions of thrones and crowns. Could anything that Jesus might *say*
to them pierce the darkness in their minds? No, but his act will speak
to them, speak to them more powerfully than any word. Silently Jesus
procures a towel and basin, puts off his coat, and is down upon his knees
washing the disciples' feet. The Son of God has become a Servant—the
Servant of the Lord. Now with his towel and basin, he is at the feet of
Judas, Judas who will soon be slipping out into the darkness to finish
his black treachery. Now he moves round to Peter. Then James and
John, Matthew and Thomas, Philip and Bartholomew, and all the rest.

The acted parable is over, and Jesus, taking his garments, is again at
the table's head. 'If I then have washed your feet,' he says, 'you also
ought to wash one another's feet, for I have given you an example.'

What does this mean? That we who are Christ's disciples today, as
they were then, must literally repeat his action? No, this would be to
confuse the letter with the spirit. The example Christ set them, and sets

us, is one of humble service. Our Lord's donning of the slave's apron, his taking of the towel, proclaimed in a way that words could not, that what had formerly been the badge of slavery was to be henceforward the badge of the highest and holiest service, the badge of the only Kingdom which is divine—

> Its King a Servant, and its sign
> A gibbet on a hill.

Not crowns and coronets but towels and basins are the insignia of the Saviour's Kingdom, and he best honours the Son of God who is prepared to stoop and serve.

It is a hard lesson for our human pride to learn. Have we Christians learned it even yet?

III

'He took a loaf.'

The third, the last, the greatest of his Action Sermons, and one that has reverberated down the centuries and round the world. We need not paint the background—it is too familiar. Once again Christ chooses one of earth's commonest things to teach his heavenly truth. Only a loaf of bread, we say. Ah, but we think too meanly of bread. For, besides being 'the staff of life', the mere eating of bread has been, from time immemorial, the symbol of true friendship. When, therefore, our Lord 'took a loaf', was he simply preaching a sermon on the golden text of friendship? Far from it! This was *broken* bread. 'He took a loaf—and broke it,' we read. 'This is my body broken for you,' he said. 'As it happens to this loaf, so it is happening to me.' It is this word over the loaf which puts atonement into what happened, a few hours later, outside a city wall. 'Take, eat,' he commanded his disciples, and the eating which followed is far more than a simple sequel to the action sermon. 'It is the gift of a share,' said Rudolf Otto, 'a share in the power of the broken Christ.' It is as if Christ were saying, 'Eating this broken bread, you are entering into God's redeeming purpose. You are making your own all that God is doing through my death for a world's redemption.' Even so, nineteen centuries later, we 'take and eat'. No more than the first disciples may we fathom all the deep mysteries of the Saviour's Passion, for

> None of the ransomed ever knew
> How deep were the waters crossed,

but their Lord is our Lord, now risen from the dead and alive and reigning for ever. We believe that he was 'broken' for us; that, as we fulfil his command, he comes to us to be the meat and drink of our souls; and that he is able to save to the uttermost all who come to God through him:

> And so we come: O draw us to thy feet,
> Most patient Saviour, who canst love us still,
> And by this food, so awful and so sweet,
> Deliver us from every touch of ill:
> In thine own service make us glad and free
> And grant us nevermore to part with thee.

XI

THE LORD'S PRAYER

'Pray then like this'—Matt. 6.9 (RSV).

I N a letter written shortly before he died, Thomas Carlyle tells how he
whiled away a sleepless night by trying to think out the meaning of the
Lord's Prayer, only to find himself being carried out of his spiritual
depth and swept away into the ultimate mysteries. If that happened to
Carlyle, no doubt it may happen to us too; but isn't it worth while to
spend at least one sermon-time making the same attempt?

The plan of the prayer is very simple. At the beginning, an Invocation; at the end, a Doxology; and in between, six petitions. Three of
them are for the greater glory of God, and three are for our human
needs.

Look first at the Invocation—'Our Father who art in heaven.'

The important word here is 'Father'. For any religion the supreme
question is, What is God like? And for Christians there is only one
right answer, Christ's answer: God is our Heavenly Father. Not a
principle, not a force, but a Person; and not any kind of person, but a
Father. It was Jesus' way to say to his disciples: 'Think of the very best
human father you can imagine—God is all that, and far more.' Great
beyond all our comprehending, holy beyond all our conceiving, but a
Father—a Father who cares for his children, a Father who is sad when
they go astray, and glad when they come home: the Father to whom his
own life was one long and loving obedience, and to whom he committed
his spirit on the Cross. This is the God we invoke as 'our Father'. Yes,
mark the pronoun 'our'. When we say it, we join ourselves with the
whole family of God in the wide earth.

1. Now turn to the first petition—'Hallowed be thy name.'

'What's in a name?' we say, as though it were simply a label devised
for the postman's convenience. But the Bible takes names seriously. In
the Bible the name of a person stands for his nature as revealed. So
God's name is his nature, or character, as he has revealed it to us. Now
God has made his character known in many ways—in the beauty of his

created world, in his mighty acts in history, above all in his Son, Jesus Christ. How then is his name to be 'hallowed'—kept holy, reverenced? We hallow God's name in our minds, by thinking only worthy thoughts of him; in our speech, by keeping only pure and true words on our lips; and in our deeds, by doing only what he would have his children do.

2. The second petition reads 'Thy kingdom come.'

Please don't picture God's Kingdom as a politician's paradise or some kind of super Welfare State under Divine patronage. The Kingdom of God signifies God's 'Kingly Rule'. A dynamic, not a static idea! It means God reigning, God breaking decisively into history to visit and redeem his people. More than that, it is the very heart of the Gospel that God's reign really and finally began when he sent his Son, by his life and death, to reconcile the world to himself. This, however, was only a beginning; and from this unremarkable beginning, Jesus said in the Parable of the Mustard Seed, the Kingdom was destined to grow to unimaginable endings. The Kingdom then has been inaugurated, but it has not yet been consummated.

So when we pray 'Thy kingdom come', we pray God to *complete* his great purpose of salvation which he took in hand when he sent his Son.

When that Kingdom fully comes, evil will be abolished for ever, and all the promises of the Beatitudes will come true. Then the mourners will be comforted, the pure in heart will see God, and his children will be finally at home in their Heavenly Father's house.

3. Now turn to the third petition—'Thy will be done, in earth as it is in heaven.'

Only God can consummate his reign. Does this mean that man can sit back and do nothing? No, this petition reminds us that *we* have our part to play. But see what we have done with it! We have turned the words 'Thy will be done' into a tombstone *cliché*, when Jesus meant them as a summons to God's servants to be up and doing—'Thy will be done—and done by me!'

What is God's will? What pleases God. And what that is, Christ has told us. It is health, not disease; service, not selfishness; giving, not grabbing; loving, not hating; the Golden Rule, not the rule of the jungle. In God's heaven it is always so; and here we pray that earth may become in this like heaven.

So the first half of the prayer ends. Having asked for the big things, we are now free to pray for our own needs, and in particular, for provision, for pardon and for protection.

4. 'Give us this day our daily bread.' This, the fourth petition, teaches

our dependence on God. Sometimes we say that a man has 'independent means'. But nobody really has. We can't command the harvest; God gives it. And all the tractors in the world would be so much useless metal, if God didn't quicken life within the seed. No, our daily bread comes not from the farmer, not from the miller, not from the baker, but from God. And this our dependence on him we acknowledge whenever we say 'Grace before meat'.

But notice two things. First, Jesus authorizes us to ask God only for what we need. It is a prayer for daily bread, and not for daily cake! Second, this petition is not an invitation to idleness. It does not rule out the human effort needed to make God's gift our own. As somebody has remarked, 'God feeds the sparrows, but he doesn't put the crumbs into their mouths.'

5. The fifth petition says: 'And forgive us our debts, as we forgive our debtors.'

From bread to sin; for there is another hunger, the hunger of the soul for forgiveness of all the sins that separate us from God. We are all sinners; we sin every day; and every day we need to ask God's pardon.

Notice that Christ calls sins 'debts'. The word stands for all that we should do towards God and our fellow men—all that we should do and don't. So every day we must say we are sorry and ask God's forgiveness.

But mark the condition attached: 'as we forgive our debtors.' The two forgivenesses go together. We needn't pray for forgiveness if we are not ready to bestow it. An unforgiving spirit slams the door in the face of God's forgiveness. When General Oglethorpe said to John Wesley, 'I never forgive', Wesley replied, 'Then I hope, sir, you never sin.' For 'unforgiving, unforgiven' is a law of the spiritual world over which our Father rules.

6. The last petition says: 'And lead us not into temptation, but deliver us from evil.'

It is a cry for protection. But watch the word 'temptation'. Here it does not signify enticement to do evil; for God never does that. It means 'trial' or 'testing'. Now God does permit us to be tested; and without such trials we would never develop any moral muscle or back-bone. Yet every trial involves the risk that you and I may succumb to the downward pull of evil. Therefore, in this petition we pray: 'Heavenly Father, so far as it is possible, spare us moral adventures; but if they needs must be, help us to come victoriously through them.'

Then, as with a peal of trumpets, the Prayer ends in a Doxology— 'For thine is the kingdom, and the power, and the glory for ever'—and we are back where we began in the thought of the majesty and perfection of God.

Well, that is the Lord's Prayer, the Prayer Jesus taught his disciples, the family Prayer, the Prayer that teaches us how to pray. It is so short and simple that a child can understand enough to pray it. On the other hand, the saint or the sage can never fathom all its depths. Unfathomable? Yes, but how universal also! For it concerns itself with the needs of all men, high and humble, rich and poor, white and yellow and black.

The true Christian will pray it every day; and when he prays it, he should try to pray it with meaning, and with the full force of his heart.

XII

EVERYBODY'S TEXT

'God so loved the world that he gave his only Son, that whoever believes in him should not perish but have eternal life'—John 3.16 (RSV).

S OMEBODY once asked John MacNeill, the famous Scottish evangelist: 'Do you never preach from John 3.16?' 'Na, na,' said John, 'I have *that* in every sermon I preach.' Yes, this is everybody's text, and a text for every occasion. If I had only one sermon to preach, this would be my text; and I have little doubt that if a vote were taken on the greatest verse in the Bible, this one would come out first. Why? Wherein lies the appeal of John 3.16?

There are texts more obviously striking. There are texts whose literary beauty is greater. There are texts which, at first sight, carry a plainer message for Everyman in his pilgrimage. Why has this been named 'Everybody's text'?

Surely it is because the spiritual instinct of multitudes tells them that here, if anywhere, is the heart of the Gospel. This is, as Martin Luther said, 'the Gospel within the Gospels'.

This is not to deny the literary splendours of the Bible. These are unchallengeable. It is not to deny that the Bible contains a treasury of wisdom well fitted to guide men's erring footsteps through the world. But weak and sinful men and women—and that we are such the radical wrongness of our world today abundantly proves—when they go to the Bible want more than fine literature or human wisdom. They want help from higher places. They want a 'word from the Beyond for our human predicament'. They want the assurance that in all the guilt and grief with which they are beset, the almighty being whom they call God, really and veritably cares for them—nay more, has done something for this deep and radical disease of their souls.

And it is just this message—this assurance—this Word from the Beyond—which St John has written for them in words which age cannot wither nor custom stale.

1. 'God so loved the world' it begins.

I doubt if we Christians ever wonder enough at the terrific truth on which our Faith is founded—I mean, the love of God. Sometimes we sentimentalize it, forgetting that the love of the Eternal must be *holy* love, love that cannot palter with evil in any shape or form. Oftener we simply take it for granted as something obvious and self-evident, like the sun in the summer sky. Yet the love of God is emphatically not something self-evident. It is not a truth of natural religion. It is not a conclusion that any thinking man might reach, say, by studying Nature. Indeed, not a few have been so impressed—or, rather, depressed—by 'Nature red in tooth and claw', that they have repudiated it altogether. No, if we believe in the love of God, it is because of one fact, because we have glimpsed the glory of the Divine Love in the face of God's only Son, Jesus Christ, because, at the Cross, as through a window, we have seen into the heart of the Eternal.

2. 'God is love.' True, but that is not enough. Only love that authenticates itself in deeds is worthy the name of love. A man may protest his love for you in a hundred fine phrases; but if that man never lifts a finger to help you when you are in trouble, you will suspect—and rightly suspect—his love. Love must prove itself in deeds. Now it is the very heart of the Gospel that the Almighty so loved us, all unworthy as we are, that he did something, something that alone makes sense of this riddling thing we call existence, something unspeakably costly to himself.

'God gave. . . .'

Listen to the original Greek: *Hōste ton huion autou ton monogenē edōken.* Here, writes W. F. Howard, the expert on St John, is the outstanding example of the theological value of grammar. John might have written *hōste dounai* 'so as to give', to mark the measure of the potential gift. Instead he wrote *hōste edōken* 'so that he gave', to declare the magnitude of the recorded act. 'God gave.' Gave what? Gave up his only Son—gave him up to be born of woman, to take our nature upon him, to taste our griefs and temptations, and to die at last a felon's death upon a cross, through and for our sins.

We try to fathom what that gift must have cost God; and since we have no other resource, we fall back on poor human analogies. We think of Abraham offering up Isaac, or of those who have given only sons in time of war. We think, maybe, of Sir Harry Lauder's story of New York in the First World War: of a little lad and his father walking the streets of the great city; and suddenly the lad spies a star cut in a window, and asking the reason, learns that the star means that that family has given a son in the war; and how later, as the two come, in the gloaming, into the open, the lad descries a single bright star in the evening sky, and with a child's flash of insight that goes deeper than he ever dreams, cries out, 'Look, Daddy, God must have given his Son too.'

3. 'That whoever believes in him should not perish.'

Note that word 'perish', please. It has a sombre sound. We are apt to gloss over it nowadays. There's a bit of the Pharisee in most of us that makes us think we're too good to damn, or God too soft to damn us— you know, 'He's a Good Fellow, and 'twill all be well.' We have watered down the urgency of the Gospel. We have forgotten the awful alternatives with which the New Testament faces men: life—or death.

I'm not prepared to expound all that is implied in that word 'perish'. Time was when Christian preachers found it easy to bludgeon people into believing by awful threats of what was in store if they did not. Well, the old-fashioned eschatological sanctions—the fear of Hell and all the rest of it—have lost most of their terror nowadays. We need not regret it; for many of them were quite unworthy of the God and Father of our Saviour. And yet—and yet we dare not forget that Christ himself does say in solemn words that a man by deliberately rejecting him, may forfeit his chance of 'life'. 'You seem, sir,' said Mrs Adams to Dr Johnson, in one of those hours when the fear of death and judgment lay heavy upon him, 'You seem, sir, to forget the merits of our Redeemer.' 'Madame,' said the honest old man, 'I do not forget the merits of my Redeemer, but my Redeemer has said that he will set some on his right hand—and some on his left.'

4. 'That whoever believes in him should not perish, but have eternal life.'

What is 'eternal life?' Not quite the same thing as 'everlasting life' which deals in mere duration; which simply means 'going on for ever', like Tennyson's Brook. 'Eternal life' is life of a new quality, life lived in communion with God through Christ, life with the tang of eternity about it; a life that begins here and now. But let a great theologian, Emil Brunner, define it:

> To have part in the Divine Life of Jesus Christ by faith, to stand in the midst of history and be comprehended in eternal salvation, through the reconciliation made in him who is called the Life and the Way to Life—this is to be a Christian—to have life eternal.

And if you ask me to explain it further, what can I do but point you to a multitude without number, who, like St John, have found through faith in the living Christ, even in this present life with all its griefs and graves, a fellowship which transcends all earthly fellowships, a peace which this world cannot give, a love which impels them, like Saul Kane, to 'brother all the souls on earth'.

'All this—and heaven too' is eternal life. Life that is life indeed here and now; and after death, life beyond all hope of telling, wonderful. This is life eternal. This is God's gift in the Gospel. This is the reason why he gave his only Son. This is the blessedness he offers to all men.

XIII

TETELESTAI

'It is finished'—John 19.30.

As on this day, at the ninth hour—3 p.m. our time—in the year AD 30, Jesus Christ died on a Cross outside the northern wall of Jerusalem. His last utterance, according to St John, was one brief, triumphant word: *'Tetelestai!* It is finished!'

From that day to this a multitude whom no man can number and who swear eternal allegiance to that crucified Man, believing him to be Divine, have cried 'Amen' to that last ringing word of his, persuaded that when he died, the divinest work in all history had been carried to a victorious conclusion.

'Finished!' he said. But what was finished? You will find the answer in that saying which Christ uttered by the Well of Samaria: 'My meat is to do the will of him that sent me, and to finish his work.' It was God's work—the work that the Father had given him to do—which was finished upon the Cross.

What was this work? We will try to answer the question from Christ's own words—more particularly from three picture-phrases which he himself used.

1. First, then, Christ saw his Passion and Death as a *cup* to be drunk.

'Can you drink of the cup that I am drinking?' he said to James and John. 'O my Father, if it be possible, let this cup pass from me,' he prayed in the Garden of Gethsemane.

A cup? What did Christ mean by this cup which the Father had given him? As a rule, we use the word for some joyful experience, saying in hours of great happiness, 'My cup is filled to overflowing.' But in the Bible a cup more often signifies some bitter experience. It represents a lot appointed by God—and that lot generally one of affliction. It is a cup of anguish and woe. And such, beyond all doubt, was the cup of which Christ spoke.

Was it then the actual physical pain of the Cross—the pain of death by crucifixion—which was uppermost in his mind when he used the word? Nay verily. To be sure, death by crucifixion was cruel enough in all conscience—*crudelissimum teterrimumque supplicium*, says Cicero, 'cruellest and foulest of punishments'; yet hundreds before Christ had endured it bravely. There is more to it than physical pain. Surely James Denney is right when he says: 'It is hard to believe that it was simply the anticipation of pain which made Christ cry "O my Father, if it be possible, let this cup pass from me." It was the anticipation of that experience when, all sinless as he was, the Father would put into His hands the cup our sins had mingled.'

'The cup our sins had mingled.' This was the cup Christ had to drink. So closely had he associated himself with those he came to save—in Maltby's phrase, so irrevocably had he betrothed himself to the human race for better, for worse—that Christ tasted, in all its horror, the wrath of God against the sin of man; and for one dread moment during the agony it seemed as if the cup would prove too bitter for him—

> A voice upon the midnight air
> Where Kidron's moonlit waters stray
> Weeps forth in agony of prayer:
> 'O Father, take this cup away!'
> 'Ah, Thou who sorrowest unto death,
> We conquer in Thy mortal fray,
> And earth for all her children saith:
> "O God, take not this cup away!" '

It was not taken away. He had to drink it in all its bitterness, even to enduring on the Cross that awful sense of separation from God which wrung from him the most desolating cry in history, 'My God, my God, why hast thou forsaken me?' But he drank it to the dregs; and when he died, he knew the cup was empty. 'It is finished.' Whatever else that saying means, it means that when Christ died, he had drained the cup his Father had given him, the cup our sins had mingled.

2. Secondly, Christ saw his Passion as a *road* to be travelled. 'The Son of man goeth as it is written of him,' he said, foretelling his death. We might fill out the saying thus: 'The Son of man is travelling the road mapped out for him in Scripture.' And if we ask what road in Scripture he means, there can be but one answer. It is that *via dolorosa*, that path of shame and death, mapped out centuries before, in the fifty-third chapter of Isaiah—the chapter which tells of the Suffering Servant of God, despised and rejected of men, who 'bare the sin of many, and made intercession for the transgressors'.

Of course, it is a road of the spirit which Christ knew he had to travel;

yet as we read the Gospels, we see how it leads Christ through one actual place after another in Galilee and Judea. It begins at the Baptism, on the banks of Jordan; it winds through that barren Wilderness near the Dead Sea where he was tempted to swerve aside from the sombre way appointed for him and to take the broad easy highway of the world and of the devil; it takes a decisive turning-point at Caesarea Philippi when 'he sets his face steadfastly to go to Jerusalem'. From that point onwards, the road slopes down into the dark valley till, at the lowest descent thereof, there falls across his path, stark and appalling, the shadow of a Cross. Yet on he presses, resolute and unflinching, on to the end of the road—

On to the city of God—

till with the long last mile behind him and the Hill of Calvary climbed he can cry at journey's ending, 'It is finished! I have travelled the road!'

3. Last of all, Christ saw his Passion as a *price* to be paid. 'The Son of man,' he said, 'came not to be served but to serve and to give his life a ransom for many.'

A ransom for many . . . a price to be paid. What does this mean? Dead seas of ink have been expended on this great saying, and every word of it has been studied and weighed by the scholars. Yet after all their study no one has ever fathomed all its depths—

But none of the ransomed ever knew
How deep were the waters crossed.

Yet whatever else it means, it means this at least, that by their sin the lives of the many had become forfeit, and that Christ knew himself called by the sacrifice of his own sinless life, to release them from the doom which overhung them. A price had to be paid, and that price the life of the only Son of God—

There was no other good enough
To pay the price of sin.

So Christ conceived his work; so he set himself to fulfil it through tears and bloody sweat; so, at the last, when he hung dying on the Cross, he knew that the awful price had been paid, and with his triumphant *tetelestai* he gave up his soul to God.

'It is finished.' In Christ's own picture-phrases this means: 'I have drained the cup. I have travelled the road. I have paid the price.' Metaphors all of them, no doubt; perhaps only in metaphors could our Lord describe his work ere it was done. But the work was finished, and of the results of that finished work Christians down the centuries have never doubted.

A well-known picture at Catterick Camp painted during the First World War shows a signaller lying dead in No-man's-land. He had been sent out to repair a cable broken by shell-fire. There he lies cold in death but with his task fulfilled. For in his stiffening hands he holds together the cable's broken ends. Beneath the picture is the one word 'Through'.

That is a picture-parable of what Christians believe about the finished work of Jesus Christ. Sin had snapped the contact between God and man. Christ by his death had brought the broken ends together, had restored the broken fellowship between God and man.

> O love of God! O sin of man!
> In this dread act your strength is tried,
> And victory remains with love;
> Jesus, our Lord, is crucified!

XIV

THE UNFADING VICTORY

'Thanks be to God which giveth us the victory'—I Cor. 15.57.

THIS is V-Day in the Church. Today we commemorate the greatest victory in history. The Resurrection of Christ is the greatest victory in history because, while the victories of other conquerors—your Alexanders, Caesars, Napoleons and Hitlers—grow old and fade from the memories of men, this victory abides. It abides, because the Victor abides. 'Christ, being raised from the dead, dieth no more. Death hath no more dominion over him.'

'We sing the praise of him who died,' and rightly. On the Cross, Christ died, by his Father's appointing, to ransom men from their sins. But the Cross is really a terrific question-mark against the sky. If the Story of Jesus ends there, we are still, as Paul said, 'in our sins'; there is no good and loving heavenly Father at the heart of things; and we are 'of all men most miserable'. But, thanks be to God, the Story does not end at the Cross. The Cross does not stand alone. Cross and Resurrection are but two aspects of one great redeeming Act of God, the second of which illumines, as with a great shaft of light, the darkness of the first. Easter Day is the interpretation of Good Friday. The Resurrection is the making manifest by miracle of the victory of God's saving purpose which took Christ to the Cross. It is the Father's seal set on his Son's sacrifice. We do well to fix our gaze on Calvary; but we never see it aright until we see it with the light of the first Easter morning breaking behind that Cross upon the lonely hill.

Lift up your hearts, then, this Easter Day and think with me of the Resurrection as a fact, an experience, and a hope.

I

The Resurrection of Christ is, first, a fact of history. If I did not believe this, I would never enter a pulpit again. Once in history one man left a gaping tomb in the wide graveyard of the world, and this victory is like the breach in a North Sea dyke, an event of apparently small importance whose consequences are incalculable. 'Yes, yes,' you say, 'but how long ago it was! Is the thing really true?'

Well, all I can do is to give you my opinion, as one whose job it is to know it, that the evidence is to be trusted. It is both abundant and impressive. The very earliest evidence of all—that in I Cor. 15.3 ff.—goes back to within a few years of the event itself. It goes back to a time when there were literally hundreds still living who, with their own eyes, had seen Christ risen and alive, so that St Paul can say, in effect, 'If you don't take my word for it, ask them. They saw him risen, and the event changed their whole lives.'

Further, remember that that evidence has been weighed and sifted as no other evidence has ever been weighed and sifted. Yet, when all tests have been applied, two things in it stand out unshaken:

1. Joseph of Arimathea's rock-tomb had lost its tenant.
2. Christ appeared alive to many people and talked with them.

Now, it is open to you if you want to be a sceptic, to try to find other 'explanations' for these two facts. Many have tried it, but their explanations have been singularly unconvincing. Even if the sceptic could explain away the empty tomb and the appearances of Christ, there would still remain certain other stubborn facts which make no sense—unless the Christian claim is true.

The silence of the Jews is one of them. For them, Jesus was an impostor who had died the death he deserved. Yet not many days after this impostor's followers were making Jerusalem ring with the news that he had risen. Clearly, if the Jews could have shown this news to be false, they would have done so. But they did not. Why? Because they could not.

The second fact is the change in the disciples. Cowards had become heroes, almost overnight. Only the Resurrection will explain why men who, at Calvary, 'all forsook him and fled', were ready, a week later, to face any danger for his sake.

Finally, there is the evidence of the Church. For make no mistake: it was on the Resurrection that the Church was built. If the life of Jesus had ended on the Cross, he might have been remembered for a few years as a good and brave man, but, with the lapse of time, he would soon have been forgotten. But what did happen? The very opposite! After his death there sprang into existence a body of men who went forth to proclaim the risen Christ to the ends of the earth: a body of men who still worship him and adore him. Only the fact of the Resurrection will explain the existence—and the persistence—of the Church. But the fact does not stand alone. There is the experience.

II

I mean the experience of the living Christ. When Christ arose from the dead, he did not rise to the old life—he passed into a different mode of being. He passed from this to the spiritual world. But did this mean that he had forsaken his own? On the contrary! He became to them more real than ever. He came back to them as a spiritual presence: he was with them; he lived in them.

You remember Denney's paradox: 'No apostle ever remembered Christ.' No, they had no need to. He was still with them, unseen but not unknown. He stood by them in their dangers. He was with them when they broke the bread.

This is what I mean by the Resurrection as experience. And it is not something that only the first Christians enjoyed. It is an experience that may be ours also—

> Shakespeare is dust and will not come
> To question from his Avon tomb;
> And Socrates and Shelley keep
> An Attic and Italian sleep. . . .
>
> They see not. But, O Christians who
> Throng Holborn and Fifth Avenue,
> May you not meet, in spite of death,
> A Traveller from Nazareth?

In every age Christ's followers give the same glad testimony. 'Jesus Christ came to me in my cell last night' says Samuel Rutherford of his Aberdeen gaol; and three centuries later Charles Raven records a like encounter in a Midland slum. 'Christ is alive, as alive as I am myself, cries Dr Dale in his Birmingham study as the reality of the risen Lord comes on him like 'a burst of sudden glory'. 'I have had personal dealings with the risen Christ as my Saviour,' testifies P. T. Forsyth, 'nearer and dearer than my own flesh and blood.' 'He comes to us', writes Albert Schweitzer, 'as of old he came to them by the Lakeside; and he speaks to us the same word, Follow me!' It is the testimony of Christ's own in every time.

III

But, finally, the Resurrection is a hope—our hope. 'Because I live,' said Jesus, 'you shall live also.' Or, as St Paul puts it, the Christian hope is that those who are 'in Christ' now will one day be 'with Christ' for ever.

The Gospel is not a promise of 'pie in the sky when you die' to all and sundry. It does not proclaim that all men will automatically go to heaven. But it does proclaim that Christ is a living and universal Lord, that by faith and love we may be made one with him as the twig is grafted into the tree, and that, thus united with him, we too may hope to vanquish 'the last enemy' and to share his deathless life.

Therefore, in a world where so many things are shaken, I invite you this Easter Day to build your faith on the things which cannot be shaken and especially on the fact of a living Christ. 'Realize a living Christ,' says Forsyth, 'and he will produce in you a living faith. Visit his holy sepulchre in scripture, and as you pore and wait, he will surprise you from behind with his immortal life.'

Let no man, then, rob you of your Easter hope. Hold fast to your Risen Saviour. Strive to be what every Christian Church should be—a Community of the Resurrection. And take to yourselves the noble words of the Apostle:

Wherefore, my beloved brethren, be ye steadfast, unmoveable, always abounding in the work of the Lord, forasmuch as ye know that your labour is not in vain in the Lord.

XV

CHRISTIANITY AS CARING

'He careth for you'—I Peter 5.7.
'Take care of him'—Luke 10.35.

I T's the little words—staccato words like 'sin', haunting words like 'home', ultimate words like 'God'—that take you furthest into the secret of the Faith. That little word 'caring', for example. Use it as your key, and it will take you further into the meaning of Christianity than many a stout volume of theology. For what is the Gospel if it is not this, that God has cared for us in Christ—cared for us past all our deserving. And what is the Christian way of life—what we call 'the Christian Ethic' —if it is not caring, caring for other people because God has cared for us? 'Christianity' said Baron Von Hügel to his niece on his death-bed, 'Christianity taught us to care. Caring is the greatest thing. Caring matters most.'

I

Consider, to begin with, this thing we call the Gospel. Translate the theologians' big words—Incarnation, Atonement, Resurrection and the rest—translate them into words of one syllable, and what do they come to? Isn't it to this, that the great invisible Being whom we call God so cared for us, poor creatures of a day, that he gave his only Son to save us —save us from our sin, save us into fellowship with himself, both here and hereafter?

'Caring . . .' A little word of two syllables, a word that any child can grasp; and yet it stands for what Karl Barth has called 'a vertical miracle' —the coming down of the Divine Carer into this fallen world, for us men and for our salvation. And what is the Cross but the supreme proof of it all, the proof that the great Carer so cared about us men and our sinning that he came right down into our human situation at its most sinful and took the burden of it on his own shoulders: 'God was in Christ reconciling the world to himself'?

This is how William Temple once put it: Men say, 'There cannot be a God of love, because if there were, and he looked upon this world, his heart would break.'

The Church points to the Cross, and says: 'His heart *does* break.'

Men say, 'It is God who has made the world. It is he who is responsible, and it is he who should bear the load.'

The Church points to the Cross, and says: 'He *does* bear it.'

Yes, the Cross tells us how God cares. But what is the Resurrection but the shining proof that the caring did not stop there, that the sacrifice of the Cross was not in vain? What does the gift of the Holy Spirit mean but that God did not leave the world on the first Easter Day, but is still with us through his Spirit, still caring for us, still saying in our hearts, 'You are not orphans. I am still with you, to help you, strengthen you, guide you.' And what does the Christian Hope mean but that the God who cared, and cares, for us, will care for us for ever—care for us till past all darkness, danger and death, we shall see him 'face to face' in that Father's house with many rooms where Jesus has gone to prepare a place for us?

The Gospel—what is it? It is the Good News of how God cared, and cares, and will care. My friends, in face of all your doubts and difficulties, hold on to that. There is so much in our world today which leads men to despair of ever finding a meaning in the 'cosmic process'. Man's inhumanity to man, the awful incidence of war in our time, the suffering of innocent people and all the pitiful heart-ache of the world, the brooding fear that man with his new-found nuclear knowledge may well blow the world sky-high any day—these things drive many to scepticism and despair—

> My son, the world is dark with griefs and graves,
> So dark that men cry out against the stars.

Yes, but for those of us who have truly seen the meaning of the Incarnation, the Cross, the Resurrection, there is a radiant shaft of light cleaving the encircling gloom. Sin and suffering may still remain mysteries, not to be finally solved this side of eternity; but we who know what the Cross signifies—the forgiveness of sin—we who know beyond any peradventure that God raised Christ from the dead—the living Pledge of Everlasting Life—we know that God cares. And because we know that he cares, we know too that the age-long struggle between good and evil is not going to drag on for ever, but must end, one day, in the final defeat of evil and the complete victory of God and good.

II

God cared—and cares. This is the *indicative* mood which lies at the heart of the Gospel. But it carries with it, as corollary, an *imperative* mood. Christians are called to care. Caring has ever been the mark of the Christian man, as caring has been the badge of all God's greatest servants: from Francis of Assisi renouncing riches in order to care for the poor, to Father Damien betrothing himself to the leper's cause, even unto death; yes, and to our own Eric Liddell forsaking 'the glittering prizes of the track' to take the Gospel to China, or to Albert Schweitzer turning his back on Europe at the age of thirty, in order to care for his black brothers in the swamps of primeval Africa: these and a host of others unknown to fame or the history books—doctors, nurses, teachers, ministers, missionaries and the rest—all dedicated to the high task of caring for men and women in their misery, sickness, ignorance and sin.

We are called to care. There is a slogan current today which cynically proclaims: 'I couldn't care less.' Let us have no truck with it. It is quite unchristian. Its real name is callousness. It is the sin of the priest and the Levite in the parable who 'passed by on the other side'. It is the sin of Dives in the other parable—Dives who went to Hell simply because he never gave a thought to Lazarus lying in misery on his door-step—because he didn't care.

And the sin of Dives, alas, isn't only in the Bible; it is still with us. It infects the family—you get parents who ought to be denied the privilege of parenthood, so little do they care for their children. That's why you get so many juvenile delinquents.

It infects the community—you get the people of whom T. S. Eliot has written—

> dispersed on ribbon roads
> And no man knows or cares who his neighbour is,
> Unless his neighbour makes too much disturbance.

And it infects the Church—how it infects it!—you get scores of people nominally Christians, who call the Church in for wedding or for funeral but who will not even trouble to send their children to the Sunday School and who, so far as the Kingdom of God is concerned, care less about the Gospel and the Church than they do about their weekly football coupon or their weekly game of bridge.

What we need today is people who will care—and not leave it all to the Welfare State: people who care about family life and the children God has given them; people who care about the community and the fair land and liberties they enjoy; people who care that the will of God shall be done in our midst, and in our time.

What does the world need today? People who will care. And the call comes to us first, simply because we are Christians; for as Baron Von Hügel said, and I end as I began,

Christianity taught us to care. Caring is the greatest thing. Caring matters most.

XVI

RECALL TO FUNDAMENTALS

'God was in Christ'—II Cor. 5.19.
'Christ died for our sins'—I Cor. 15.3.
'Wherefore God highly exalted him'—Phil. 2.9.

LAST century, there lived in Glasgow an old woman of Covenanting stock who, when her minister, Dr Norman Macleod of the Barony, used to visit her, would confront him with her ear-trumpet and demand: 'Gang ower the fundamentals, Doctor, gang ower the fundamentals.' But what are the fundamentals?

In one of his letters to Sir William Robertson Nicoll, the great Scottish theologian James Denney wrote these words:

'I do not believe that the Christian religion, let alone the Christian Church, can live, unless we can be sure of three things—a real being of God in Christ, the atoning death, and the exaltation of Christ.'

These were, for Denney, fundamentals—the articles of a standing or falling Church. Let us go over them today.

I

'A real being of God in Christ.' This is the first essential of an enduring Christianity. For mark this well. Unless God really was in Christ, we have no Good News for a sin-sick world, no Word from the Beyond for our human predicament. If Jesus was not, in a real sense, 'God manifest in the flesh', God wearing the home-spun of our human nature, but only one more fallible man like ourselves, guessing and groping after God, we had better erase the word 'Gospel' from our vocabulary and close our churches. We are no better than the Unitarian preacher who went to Aberdeen and for three days and nights sought to win converts from the down-and-outs. On the third evening, a fallen woman out of the crowd bluntly told him that he had better pack up and go home. 'Your rope', she explained, 'is not long enough for the likes o' me.'

That poor, untutored woman knew by instinct that no mere man, not even a super-man, but only 'the Man from heaven' could meet the depth of her human need.

H

'A real being of God in Christ.' Ah, but that may suggest the Virgin Birth, and some of you have doubts about that? Then let me reassure you. 'A real being of God in Christ' is *not* tied to belief in that doctrine. The Divinity of Christ is consonant with it; but it does not depend on it. If we believe that our Lord was Divine, it is not primarily because we believe him to have been Virgin-born, but because he has worked, and works, on the human heart and on history, as only God can work.

'A real being of God in Christ'—this is the first fundamental. The only Christianity with a future is one which declares that in Christ the great God himself intervened in human history for us men and for our salvation, one which is persuaded with Paul's persuasion that God was, uniquely and decisively, in Christ.

II

'Christ died for our sins.' The second fundamental is the atoning death of Christ. Any Christianity which hopes to survive must make the Cross central.

You might think this so obvious as to be scarcely worth saying. But, alas, it is not so. Still, as of old, the Cross is a stumbling-block to many, Christians as well as non-Christians.

To some, the Cross suggests primitive ideas of a blood-thirsty deity; to others it conjures up words like 'sin' and 'judgment'—and of course enlightened modern man isn't worrying about these outmoded fictions; and others think forgiveness an easy thing—they say with Heine, 'God will forgive me—that's his business.'

So they get rid of the Cross and make the blood of Jesus of no effect.

What shall we say in answer? Why this first: so to treat the Cross is to fly in the face of the whole New Testament. As a leaf is threaded through and through with fibres, so is the New Testament threaded through with that death on the Cross. That 'Christ died for our sins' was the first article in the earliest Christian creed. On the Cross (said those first Christians) Christ had died, by his Father's appointing, to remove the barrier that separates sinful men from the holy God, to restore the broken communications between God and men. And so for them all the Cross was 'the hiding-place of God's power and the inspiration of all Christian praise'.

Study St Paul, the noblest Christian of them all. What was the Gospel's heart for him if it was not the power of the living Crucified? And no wonder: he had seen for himself, times without number, how men sunk in sin and despair could gain forgiveness and new life by trusting to that Christ and his Cross. And all down the Christian centuries men have risen up to add their testimony to his. The discovery that Christian made when he came up with the Cross, that the burden of his sins rolled away into the empty tomb, to be seen no more—this has been endlessly authenticated. What Cornish miners and Kingswood colliers testified in the eighteenth century—

> He breaks the power of cancelled sin,
> He sets the prisoner free—

thousands upon thousands have found true.

Shall we then say that the Cross is otiose, superfluous, dispensable? Let me answer with another question. Is there any other hope for the man who longs to have dominion over his sin and to get right with God? Will all the education in the world—all the science—all the psychology heal his soul's deep hurt? Can Sigmund Freud do it, or Bertrand Russell, or Dr Bronowski?

No! If you take the Cross out, you take the 'red-ripe' from the Gospel's heart, you declare that Christ's travail was in vain, and you deny to sinful man the one great, proved, historic fountain of forgiveness and new life.

III

'Wherefore God highly exalted him.' The third essential of an enduring Christianity is the exaltation of Christ. What does this mean?

It means a Christ who is now at the right hand of God, a Christ who —whether men believe it or not—is now reigning over the Church and the world: not sitting solemnly superannuate in heaven like some retired and cloistered emperor, but watching over his People, directing them, inspiring them, through the power of the Holy Spirit.

And I say that a Christianity which does not keep sounding this note of a regnant Christ is in grave peril of degenerating into an arid antiquarianism, into a lifeless groping among the dead and dusty facts of ancient history. For the Christian religion is the religion of those who worship a Christ who now lives and reigns and will one day be unveiled in his full glory.

Dr John Brown, author of *Rab and his Friends*, tells how he once heard his father preaching on the second psalm: 'Why rage the heathen?' Pushing up his spectacles and aside his papers, the old man cried to the people, 'Where is Jesus now? And where are these priests and rulers now? Jesus has gone up, and has sat down, and shall for ever sit on the throne of the universe. Where they are now, whether in heaven or in hell, I know not. But this I do know that, wherever they are, they are and for ever shall be at, or under, his feet.'

Christus regnat! Christ reigns! That is the authentic Christian note, the note that the first Christians never tired of striking, the note so dear to our Reformed forefathers, the note which our Christian brethren on the Continent recaptured once again during the Hitler tyranny, the note which any Christian Church loses at its peril, the note of the Kingship of Christ.

My friends, in a world where men fumble and falter amid perplexities and doubts, a world where many panic at the possible shape of things to come, let us who are Christians try to rise to the full height of our Christian faith.

A real being of God in Christ, the atoning Cross, and the Kingship of Christ—these are the themes of an enduring Christianity. No others find better warrant in the New Testament. No others are big enough to meet the needs of a broken world. Make them your own; build your faith on them; recall them when the bleak moods come over you; and carry them with you into your work in the world.

> God was in Christ.
> Christ died for our sins.
> Christ reigns, and shall reign for ever and ever.

XVII

THE HOLY FIRE

'I am come to send fire on the earth'—Luke 12.49.

1. Do you remember the Greek fable about Prometheus—the man who stole fire from heaven and brought it to mortal men? Jesus here proclaims himself the new, the true Prometheus sent by his Father to set the Divine Fire blazing in the world.

Fire has ever been a symbol for the Divine Presence and Power. Think of Moses, in the lone Midian desert, finding God in a bush that burned, or of the pillar of fire that guided wandering Israel in the wilderness. Or think of the prophet Jeremiah describing the Word of God committed to him as 'a burning fire shut up in his bones'. Turn to the New Testament, and it is the same story. John the Baptist prophesies of his great Successor, 'He shall baptize you with the Holy spirit and with fire.' He appears, and his word is, 'I am come to send fire on the earth.' And when he has run his course and finished his work, the Holy Spirit falls on his disciples, at Pentecost, in 'tongues like as of fire'.

'I am come to send fire on the earth,' said Jesus, 'and how I wish it were already kindled! But [he added] I have a baptism to be baptized with, and how am I straitened [cramped] until it is all over!' Notice the word 'baptism' here—it refers to Calvary, his baptism by blood. And what he means is this:

'My mission is to kindle the Divine Fire among men. O that this Fire were even now burning in the world! But before this can be, I must go the way of the Cross, for only by my dying can the Fire be kindled. That past, I shall be liberated from my wider work, and the Fire will blaze for men's redeeming.'

If this is sound interpretation—if it truly reflects the mind of Christ—then the Day of Pentecost, the day when the Holy Spirit came with power on the apostles, is the day when our Lord's wish came true. On that day, as Bengel said, 'the fire *was lit*'.

2. Yes, the Fire was lit, and has burned from that day to this. Nay, we can say more. Through nineteen centuries, whenever the Gospel has

been faithfully preached, and Christ, who is its living embodiment, been accepted as Saviour, the Gospel has been a fire. And when, by the Spirit's working, it has truly come home to men, convincing them of their sin, bringing them to peace with God, and setting their feet on the way everlasting, the testimony of those who have received the Fire has been that of John Wesley on that memorable night in Aldersgate Street, when he found saving faith: '*I felt my heart strangely warmed.*'

For the Fire of the Gospel—what is it but the holy Love of God shown at Calvary? 'Let us now turn aside,' says Dora Greenwell, speaking of the Cross, 'and look upon this great sight, of Love that burneth with fire, and is not consumed.' It is God's holy passion for man's redeeming shown once for all in Christ's sacrifice and now shed abroad in our hearts through the Holy Spirit which is 'the life of God in the soul of man'. And the proclamation of the Divine Love which, in Christ, suffered unto blood for us men and for our forgiveness—this surely is heart-warming news for sinners in the twentieth century no less than in the first: news that is still able, as Billy Graham and others have shown, to move men to repentance and to decision for new life.

There never has been, there never will be, a time when such news is not music to weary ears. God comes in it, saying to the distracted folk of this fear-ridden world: 'You are sinners, and need forgiveness. You are impotent, and need power. You are in darkness, and need light. Come then, I offer you Christ and the Fire of the Gospel. Take it, and it will burn the evil out of you. Take it, and it will light a new lamp of hope in your heart. Take it, and I will make you what I designed you to be, a child of mine and an heir, with Christ, of life everlasting.'

This is the gospel of the New Testament, however much down the centuries men may have adulterated it—the gospel of the Divine Prometheus who suffered not (as in the fable) to expiate his own sins, but to expiate the sins of the whole world, and who now lives for ever to save those who accept him, and walk his way and do his will. We must, of course, strive to proclaim this gospel in terms that will come home, livingly and meaningfully, to the men of today; but its essential content remains the same, as its power—its fire and its force—remain unquenched and unquenchable by the passage of the years.

3. There is one thing left to say. All true Christians are longing and praying for a real revival of religion in our time. The thing is this: as the Gospel is spiritual fire, so the secret of revival is the Burning Heart.

'Did not our heart burn within us?' said the two disciples on the Emmaus Road after the Risen Christ had made himself known to them.

What we need today is people like these—'incandescent people'—people aflame with the love of the living Lord. Cold hearts will never do it; only warm hearts will; for one burning heart sets another aflame, till the hallowed fire spreads and instead of one burning heart we have a whole fellowship—a Church—on fire!

Someone will say to me: 'But you're asking for more emotion in our religion. I follow the cold, clear light of reason and distrust all appeal to the feelings.' Well, if I am asking for more feeling, why not? Is not feeling as fundamental a part of our nature as reason? Why should we put asunder what God has joined? Why should we try to refrigerate what Christ has called 'a fire'? Are we not commanded by the Apostle to 'be fervent in spirit'—to 'maintain the spiritual glow'?

So I say: as you long for revival in the land, seek to create this fellowship of the burning heart, strive to multiply the number of those aflame with the love of the living Lord.

For what makes the heart to burn? There is a saying of our Lord found this time not in the canonical Gospels but in the writings of Origen, the Church Father: 'He that is near me,' said Jesus, 'is near the fire, and he that is far from me is far from the Kingdom.' There you have it. Nearness to Christ day by day and not merely on Sundays, nearness to him in faith, and prayer, and sacrament, and plain workaday Christian service—this is the secret of the Burning Heart. For he, and he alone, can set the flame burning, the flame that can light the world.

> O Thou who camest from above,
>   The pure celestial fire to impart,
> Kindle a flame of sacred love,
>   On the mean altar of my heart.

'I am come to send fire on the earth.' Even so, come Lord Jesus, and set our hearts aflame!

XVIII

THE SECRET OF FORTITUDE

Isaiah 28.16

In the corner of William Robertson Smith's portrait by Sir George Reid[1] stand three Hebrew words painted by Smith himself in the presence of the artist: *Hamma'min lo yachish.* They were his favourite text. The words which come from Isa. 28.16, are translated in the Authorized Version: 'He that believeth shall not make haste.' But a better modern rendering would be: 'He who really puts his trust in God shall never be rattled.'

When Isaiah spoke these words 700 years before Christ, the menace of Sennacherib the Assyrian—the same who (you remember) 'came down like the wolf on the fold'—lay heavy upon Jerusalem. But, like so many other words in the Bible, they are true for all time. 'He who really puts his trust in God shall never be rattled.' Here, I submit, is the secret of fortitude, of endurance, in every time of crisis.

I

I find their truth verified, first, in the life of Christ himself.

For all true Christians, the Lord Jesus is far more than the supreme believer in God. He is the *object* of their faith, One who stands with the Almighty Father on that side of reality we call Divine. Nevertheless, Christ is also, in the phrase of Hebrews, 'the Pioneer and Perfecter of faith', faith's Captain and its perfect embodiment.

The Gospels are full of stories to prove it—the Storm on the Lake, the Raising of Lazarus, above all, the dread arbitrament of Calvary when Christ 'hazarded all at a clap' on his faith in 'Abba, Father', so that history ever since has echoed and rung with its glorious verification on the first Easter Day. But the tale which, for me, best highlights our Lord's unflinching, unflusterable faith is that of Jairus's Daughter.

Listen to Principal Cairns describing it:

Jesus is making his way through the crowd with the father when the messengers meet him with the fatal words 'Thy daughter is dead.

---

[1] Now in Christ's College, Cambridge.

Why troublest thou the Master any further?' One may safely say that
every other human being in history would have taken that word 'dead'
as final and turned back. Nobody would have blamed him if he had
done so, and he risked his whole reputation by going on. Yet he went
on. What was death in comparison with God? That lets us see deep
into his spirit. The going on is every whit as wonderful as the wonder
which followed.

Can you conceive a better illustration of our text: 'He who really puts
his trust in God shall never be rattled?' Rightly does the Writer to the
Hebrews bid us fix our eyes on him who is the great Captain of all who,
in this world, go a-soldiering by faith.

II

Yes, and all down the Christian centuries the servants of God have
'drunk in' faith and valour from that Captain's eyes. Witness after
witness is here to show that in the day of the ordeal the secret of their
constancy was a faith in God, not unworthy to be compared with their
Captain's.

Here is Martin Luther on trial as a heretic and in grave peril of his
life. 'The Pope's little finger,' cries the Cardinal legate, 'is stronger than
all Germany. Do you expect your princes to take up arms to defend you?
No! And where will you be then?' 'Then as now,' replies Luther, 'in
the hands of Almighty God.'

Or, here is Andrew Melville, in the tempestuous days after the
Reformation, defying, in the name of the Kirk, all the thunders of the
Regent Morton. 'There will never be quietness in this country,' thunders the Regent, 'till half a dizzen of you be hangit, or banished the
country.' 'Tush, sir,' replies Melville, 'threaten your purple minions in
that way. It is all one to me whether I rot in the air or underground.
The earth is the Lord's, and it will not lie in your power to hang or
exile his truth.'

Or here, finally, three centuries later, is Edward Wilson of Antarctic
fame, trapped with his friend Captain Scott in that final, fatal blizzard
at the South Pole, and writing from the tent of death thus to his wife.
'Do not be unhappy. All is for the best. We are playing a good part in a
great scheme arranged by God himself, and all is well.'

Truly, he who really puts his trust in God shall never be rattled.

III

Now, leaving the past, let us descend to the present. How does our
text and its truth stand up in this day of the ordeal?

You and I are living in a world which provides excuses in plenty for panicking. Over the globe from Washington to Moscow hangs a deep spiritual depression. Guided missiles, megaton bombs and nuclear 'fallout' provide the headlines of the news, while the 'great ones of the earth' (as Christ called them) threaten each other with incineration by nuclear holocaust. Small wonder if millions of folk are scared stiff by the possible shape of things to come. (One thinks of the mother in the Panorama programme who wished the government to issue suicide pills to parents so that they might painlessly put away their children when the hydrogen bombs began to fall.)

In face of such terrors multitudes of our countrymen tend to panic. And if we ask why, the sad but true answer is that, if they have any faith at all (which thousands haven't), it falls lamentably short of what the New Testament means by the word—a faith like Paul's, for example, or St Peter's. If they had that faith, they would not be rattled.

During the First World War, when things were at their grimmest, that great Aberdonian, P. T. Forsyth, wrote a book called *The Justification of God*. It is as timely now as it was then.

The book was a 'theodicy'—a justification of the ways of God in a world where evil exists and is rampant. And this is the gist of what he said.

There is no theodicy for the world—no justification of God and his ways in it—except in a theology of the Cross. Let a man understand the Cross aright, and he will never give way to ultimate despair. For the Cross is God's key to the otherwise undecipherable riddle of history, with all its tragedies. On that Cross the only Son of God died, by his Father's appointing, for the sins of the world, so that ever since evil has been in principle judged and doomed. 'The thing is done; it is not to do.' There, at the Cross, as by some great lightning flash, the holy love of God that still judges and saves men, was eternally revealed. And therefore if war, which is sin's apocalypse, now terrifies men making them cry out 'Why does God permit such things to happen?', it is because men today have lost the insights of New Testament faith. If they had such faith and if they did but honestly acknowledge the greed and godlessness now abroad in the world, they would find it astonishing if God's judgments had *not* fallen on it.

But there is another side to the medal of God's revelation in the Cross, and it is this. If the holy God did not spare his only Son—his most precious possession—we may be sure he will spare no historical crisis or calamity needful for the establishment of his Kingdom.

Now the man who really believes this—and this is Christian faith—knows that, whatever befall—yes, even a nuclear holocaust—the world is God's, that he has the evil of it in the hollow of his hand, and that the nations which rage so furiously are still in the leash of the redeeming God.

It is to such a faith that you and I are called in face of the temptations to panic now upon us. When the hearts of men and women everywhere are failing them for fear, it is our duty as Christians to confront them with that faith which cannot be rattled because it draws all its inspiration from the ageless victory of the Cross. Armed with that faith, we can say with Forsyth:

> The evil world cannot win at last, because it failed to win the only time it ever could. It is a vanquished world in which men play their devilries. Christ has overcome it.

And his victory on the Cross is the pledge of the final victory of God. 'He who really puts his trust in God shall never be rattled.' Let us pray God to lead us ever more fully into that victorious faith.

XIX

THE UNDERPINNING ULTIMATES

II Cor. 13.14

G. K. CHESTERTON once observed that if you ever found yourself renting a room from a landlady, your first question should not be about the food or the furniture she could offer you. No, it would be far better to fix her with a steady eye and demand, 'Madam, what is your total view of the universe?'

Absurd? Well, is it? Isn't everything else in the long run quite secondary? Isn't the really important thing just 'your total view of the universe'? That is, what you believe about the ultimate realities that underpin your life. (It seems to me that the invention of the H-bomb is forcing such questions upon us with an almost terrifying urgency; and it is my prayer that the fear of science may beget in men another fear—a fear that is wholesome and not horrible—the fear of the Lord which is the beginning of wisdom.)

If you had asked St Paul what were the ultimate realities which underpinned his life, he would have answered, 'Why, the grace of the Lord Jesus Christ and the love of God and the fellowship of the Holy Spirit.'

Suppose we spend a little time thinking about them, for the words are so familiar that we seldom stop to think what they really mean.

I

'The grace of the Lord Jesus Christ.' That is the first one. What is 'grace'?

'Grace' is the English equivalent of the Greek word Paul wrote, *charis*. To begin with, *charis* meant 'that which gives pleasure'. When the old Greeks used it centuries before Christ, they liked to link it with 'loveliness'. Then came the Gospel, baptizing the word with new meaning, and henceforth 'grace' became twin sister to love. So, in the New Testament, 'grace' is just wonderful kindness, the sort of kindness that takes your breath away when you realize how little you deserve it. And 'the grace of Christ'? It is simply his wonderful kindness to sinners—

that kindness in action. As somebody has said, it is that quality in Christ by which he always comes to people when they need him. You remember how he came thus to humble people long ago in the days of his flesh— to the disciples in the storm, to the woman that was a sinner, to Zaccheus of Jericho, to all the last, the least and the lost, to the Penitent Thief?

Well, Jesus, after he had risen from the dead, made a promise, 'Lo, I am with you always.' And ever since he has been coming to men and women like that: unseen but not unknown. When Samuel Rutherford lay in his Aberdeen gaol, he testified in his diary: 'Jesus Christ came to me in my cell last night, and every stone glowed like a ruby.'

It is the witness of the saints that Christ still comes like that—

> I see Thee not, I hear Thee not,
> Yet art Thou oft with me. . . .

We all need that grace; we all may have it. That is the first divine reality underpinning your life as Christians.

II

The second is 'the love of God'. Dwell a moment on the word 'love'. Nowadays it can cover almost everything from Hollywood to heaven. Alas, we have so soiled the word by ignoble use that it is no longer a wholly satisfactory translation of the Greek word Paul wrote. That word was *agapē*; and if we want its New Testament meaning, it is often better to use the English word 'care'. Just try it out: 'God so cared for the world . . .' 'Thou shalt care for thy neighbour as thyself.' Yet, to be frank, it is not the translation but the *truth* of the phrase which perplexes many of our contemporaries. They look out on the chaos and cruelty of the world today, and they say, 'Is it true? Does God really care?'

Well, the world contains comparatively few out-and-out atheists. Most people are too sensible for that—I mean, they don't believe that the world just happened. Common sense tells them that it must have been called into existence by some kind of Power or another. The question which vexes them is: What kind of a Power? Is it good? Is it bad? Or is it just indifferent?

Now, like St Paul, we Christians have no hesitation in answering. We believe that the Power behind the universe is not a Thing but a Person, not a Fate but a Father, a Father who cares.

Why do we believe this? We believe it because of the Fact of Christ. Like St Paul, we find the clue to the riddle of the world in him. We

believe that the Supreme Being not only called the world into existence
and still keeps his controlling hand upon it—

He's got the world in his hand—

but that, once in history, he came right down into it as a Man, to show
us what he is like, and then willed to die upon a Cross, through and for
our sins, that we might know how much he cares for us. So, when we're
asked, How can you be sure of the love of God? we point to Christ: to
Christ and his teaching first, for he taught us that God cares; but above
all, to the Cross and the empty grave. 'He that hath seen me,' said Jesus,
'hath seen the Father.' We see Christ dying upon his Cross and we cry,
'God loves—like that.' We see Christ risen from the dead in all his
Easter glory, and we cry: 'Behold the omnipotent love of the Father.'

'God! Thou art love! I build my faith on that' says the poet; and so
say we. 'The love of God'—why, it's the only thing that puts a meaning
into this strange, riddling, bitter-sweet thing we call existence. The love
—the caringness—of God, shown in the blood of Calvary and in the
shining miracle of the Resurrection—that is the second spiritual fact
underpinning our lives as Christians.

III

And now this other one—'the fellowship of the Holy Spirit'.

There's an unsolved problem of interpretation here. The Greek word
for fellowship is *koinōnia* but nobody knows for certain whether Paul
meant 'the fellowship which the Holy Spirit creates' or 'fellowship in
the Holy Spirit'. But does it greatly matter? Aren't both true?

Do you find the Christian doctrine of the Holy Spirit hard to understand? Many people do. Then remember that it means, quite simply,
'God here—here and now—and not simply in the Holy Land nineteen
centuries ago.' It is, as Henry Scougal put it, 'the life of God in the soul
of man', your soul and my soul.

The Holy Spirit is the invisible power of God which, descending on
God's people on the day of Pentecost, has been working in them ever
since. Not so much God above men, or God alongside them as God
inside them. Whether you know it or not, it is the Power which prompts
every true prayer you make; the Power which helps you to confess Christ
as your Saviour and Lord; the Power which binds you with other sinners
into that saved and saving Community, which we call the Church; the
Power which inspires all true and lovely and heroic Christian living.

And every virtue we possess
And every victory won
And every thought of holiness
Are His alone.

Shall we sum it up? What are the three Divine realities underpinning the Christian's life? The answer is: the wonderful kindness of Christ the Son, the infinite care of God the Father, and the beneficent power of the Holy Spirit. Did I say three? Then I am wrong. For of course the three are one—the Holy Trinity, Father, Son and Holy Spirit, one God blessed for ever.

For nineteen centuries now millions and millions of men and women have walked through this house of their pilgrimage and gone down at last to the dark river, supported by faith in this triune God.

Will you? Then go forth in that faith, and amid all life's ills and accidents, say with that gallant soldier of the Cross, St Patrick:

I bind unto myself today
The strong name of the Trinity.

And may the wonderful kindness of Christ the Son, and the infinite care of God the Father, and the strong help of the Holy Spirit be with you, this day and for evermore.

Part Three

A THEOLOGIAN
OF NEW TESTAMENT FAITH—
P. T. FORSYTH

ABBREVIATIONS, ETC.

Since Forsyth's books sometimes have long titles, abbreviated citation of them is necessary. For those most frequently quoted in what follows, I propose the following:

G.H.F.	God the Holy Father
P.P.M.M.	Positive Preaching and the Modern Mind
P.P.J.C.	The Person and Place of Jesus Christ
W.O.C.	The Work of Christ
P.O.A.	The Principle of Authority
J.O.G.	The Justification of God
C.E.W.	The Christian Ethic of War
C. and S.	Church and Sacraments
T.L.T.N.	This Life and the Next
G.O.G.	The Grace of the Gospel as the Moral Authority in the Church

I would only add that some of Forsyth's very best writing is tucked away in journals like *The Contemporary Review, The London Quarterly Review, The Hibbert Journal* and *The Expositor*.

There are four studies of Forsyth's theology: J. K. Mozley, *The Heart of the Gospel* (1925), chapter 3; G. O. Griffith, *The Theology of P. T. Forsyth* (1948); W. L. Bradley, *P. T. Forsyth, the Man and His Work* (1952); and R. M. Brown, *P. T. Forsyth, Prophet for Today* (1952). To these add Harry Escott, *P. T. Forsyth, Director of Souls* (1948) (which reveals the beauty of Forsyth's devotional writing and supplies an anthology), and Jessie Forsyth Andrews' vivid memoir of her father prefixed to the new edition of *The Work of Christ* (1938, reprinted 1946).

XX

FORSYTH,
HIS TIMES AND HIS WRITINGS

In a recent television interview Emil Brunner, being invited to say who was the greatest of British theologians, named an Aberdonian, Peter Taylor Forsyth.

Thus 'the whirligig of time brings in his revenges'. Fifty years ago, when Forsyth was at the peak of his powers, he was a voice crying in the Liberal wilderness, and it was left to the agnostic John Morley to pronounce him 'one of the most brilliant minds in Europe'. Now history is hastening after him; all his chief books have been reprinted; and Anglican scholars (e.g. Dr Coggan, Archbishop of York) as well as American and Continental have taken the measure of his greatness.

He was one of the great men born before his time, with the insight, and the foresight, of the prophet. In an era of prosperity before two World Wars had blown sky-high the secular dogma of inevitable progress, Forsyth was doing what Barth, Niebuhr and others have done for us in an era of collapse and despair, but with this difference: whereas they are, partly at least, commenting on *faits accomplis*, Forsyth was 'seeing the invisible'. Now, at long last, his *kairos* has come.

Was Forsyth, as is commonly said, 'a Barthian before Barth'? To an Irish student who had quoted Forsyth to him, Barth is credibly reported to have replied: 'If Forsyth had not said what he said when he said it, I would have said he was quoting me.' Likeness between the two there undoubtedly is. Like Barth, Forsyth set his face against the baneful influence of Rationalism in theology (i.e. the theological temper which regards man's reason as divine and capable of scaling the highest heights of reality). Like Barth, he set the historic revelation in Christ at the very centre of his thinking. Thus he asks: 'Is there any historic spot where eternity affirms in a person the impressions of an hour, where we are given what we cannot reach, and given it on the world scale and for ever?' To which he answers: 'The eternal finality has become an historic event. There is a point of time at which time is no longer and passes into pure but concrete eternity. That point is Christ. In Christ there is a spot where we are known far more than we know, where God not only speaks but comes, not only vouches but gives.'[1] Barth might have written this. But the parallel between Barth and Forsyth breaks down at two decisive points: on the place of reason in revelation and on the primacy of the moral.[2] While Forsyth resisted Rationalism, he could never have written what Barth once wrote: 'Faith grips reason by the throat and strangles the beast.' On the contrary, Forsyth defines theology as 'faith thinking'—the Church's supernatural faith giving a rational account of itself. Again: whereas Barth's attitude to morality is negative, Forsyth held with Butler that 'morality is the nature of things'. The moral is the real, he said, and the movements of the Supreme Reality must be morally construed as they are morally revealed. Some of us hold that on both these capital issues Forsyth is much the better guide.

I

First, then, let me say something about the life of this remarkable man —enough for you to know something of his origins and his spiritual pilgrimage—where he was born and educated, where he laboured as minister and professor, how he bore himself amid the causes and controversies of his day, the men who influenced him, the figure he cut in his world, the kind of man he was.

He was born in Chapel Street, Aberdeen on 12th May 1848 and brought up in a large rambling house, still to be seen, at the corner of Marischal Street and Castlegate. His mother Elspet Macpherson was a Highland servant lass from Kingussie who had been 'left' the big house on the death of her master, Peter Taylor, a well-known citizen of Aberdeen and a staunch Congregationalist. His father, Isaac Forsyth, was a postman's son from the Cabrach hills, a loving, spiritual, bookish man, with little of this world's goods, who had to wait, Jacob-like, nine years before he could marry his sweetheart. Then he moved into the big house, and the young couple took in boarders, mostly impecunious Highland students—George Macdonald the novelist among them—who found it hard enough to pay their fees, let alone their lodgings. 'Dinna ye fash,' Mrs Forsyth would say to some penniless Highland lad, 'gin ye find the siller for your fees, I'll find ye bed and bread.'

In this frugal home Forsyth was reared. At his baptism he received as Christian names those of his mother's benefactor. But, though desperately poor, his was a happy childhood spent on the banks of Dee and

[1] *J.O.G.*, 46 f.   [2] N. H. G. Robinson, *Exp. Times* 44 (Dec. 1952).

Don and around the quayside of Aberdeen. 'I was brought up by the sea,' he said. 'A mile or two inland, at dead of night, when all was quiet, I used to hear the sea singing a lullaby to the fisher children on the shore beneath the moon and her family of stars.'

His schooling he received at Aberdeen Grammar School where, sixty years before, Lord Byron had been a pupil; and if you visit the school today, you may see inscribed on the academic roll of honour: 'Dux for 1864: Peter T. Forsyth.'

In the autumn of that year he went up to Aberdeen University to study the classics and, like 'Shon Campbell'—'To dive in Bain and Drew.' Bain was the notable Aberdeen philosopher from whose lectures Forsyth gained an interest in Hegel, Kant and others. Eventually he took a brilliant 'first' in classics and for one year assisted the Professor of Latin. But he was destined for the Church; and in 1872, on the advice of his friend Robertson Smith, he went for a semester to Göttingen to sit at the feet of Ritschl, then the lodestone for aspiring theological students. There he learned German, and acquired a life-long interest in German theology.

On returning to England, he entered Hackney College, London. But his health was already so fragile, and his abilities so evident, that he was allowed to leave in 1874 before completing his course. After some ten years of preparation he was about to begin a career of which twenty-five years were spent in the working ministry and twenty as a professor.

Theologically, he began as an out-and-out Liberal. As the years went by, he moved, as we shall see, from this Left-wing Liberalism to Ritschlianism and then under the influence of his 'conversion' and his reading of Maurice and Dale to a neo-orthodoxy of a very vital and evangelical kind.

In 1876 he began his ministry at Shipley, a suburb of Bradford, among the working men of Yorkshire, soon acquiring a reputation as a very unorthodox preacher in a church which the local Congregational union refused to recognize. From Shipley, four years later, he moved to St Thomas's Square, Hackney, London, where he collected a congregation of 'heretics and suspects', shocked the prim by preaching in shepherd's-plaid trousers and sporting a brilliant tie, and began to take a live interest in politics, art, music and the theatre.

When in 1885 he began his third pastorate at Cheetham Hill in North Manchester, he again plunged into public life, lecturing to the working men on art and forming a friendship with G. F. Watts, the painter. His interest in children, strong all his life, showed itself in the publication (with J. A. Hamilton) of a book bearing the title *Pulpit Parables for Young Hearers*. (Later in life, when the talk turned one day to children's hymns and somebody expressed his admiration for the lines—

> I would be treated as a child
> And guided where I go,

Forsyth suggested as a great improvement—

> I would be guided as a child
> And *treated* where I go.)

In 1888 he moved to Clarendon Park, Leicester where for six years besides his work as a minister he took an active part in local politics. Here, in an essay which he contributed to a book called *Faith and Criticism* (1893), he gave the first proof of his coming power as a theologian. The essay fell under the eye of Dale of Birmingham. 'Who is this P. T. Forsyth?' he said; 'he has recovered for us a word we had all but lost—the word "grace".'

When in 1894 the call came to his last pastorate in Emmanuel Church, Cambridge, it found him in wretched health. A week after his arrival his wife (Minna Magness) died, so that for the next three or four years he lived alone with his schoolgirl daughter Jessie; and when in 1895 his *Alma Mater*, Aberdeen University, made him a Doctor of Divinity, he was too weak to go north to receive the degree in person.

Next year his famous sermon before the Congregational Union at Leicester, entitled 'The Holy Father', made the public aware that they had to reckon with a new Forsyth. On the levity of Liberalism he had turned his back for ever; henceforward his themes were to be the holiness of God, the sinfulness of sin and the power of the redeeming Cross. Nevertheless, what evidence we have suggests that the radical change in his life, of which this was the outward sign, had come some years earlier. If his was a slow rather than a sudden conversion, it had permanent results. Always reticent about it, he did once, years later, lift the veil a little:

> There was a time when I was interested in the first degree with purely scientific criticism. Bred among academic scholarship of the classics and philosophy, I carried these habits to the Bible, and I found in the subject a huge fascination, in proportion as the stakes were much higher. But, fortunately for me, I was not condemned to the mere scholar's cloistered life. I could not treat the matter as an academic quest. I was in a relation of life, duty and responsibility for others. I could not contemplate conclusions without asking how they would affect these people and my word to them in doubt, death, grief

and repentance. . . . It pleased God also by the revelation of His holiness and grace, which the great theologians taught me to find in the Bible, to bring home to me my sin in a way which submerged all the school questions in weight, urgency, and poignancy. I was turned from a Christian to a believer, from a lover of love to an object of grace.[1]

Though Forsyth for ever repudiated his old Liberal theology, he wisely retained all that was best in Liberal methods, in particular the freedom to study the Bible with the aid of the best modern scholarship. But he had become a new man in Christ, as he felt himself henceforth in his studies continually being 'corrected and humiliated by the Holy Spirit'.

Later he was to speak rather mordantly of those academic scholars who had been his first love. Their fault, as he diagnosed it, was not lack of the scholar's techniques but of a knowledge of real life. Through his work in the ministry and his contact with the manifold problems of the world, he had turned his back on all mere theology of the schools. His thinking, once done on the balcony, had moved out on to the road, had become realistic and existential. Small wonder that of all the great Christian thinkers who engaged his attention—Luther, Calvin, Kierkegaard, Maurice, Dale—his first and greatest master was the apostle Paul.

During the first three of his seven years in Cambridge his health was very precarious; but his marriage to Bertha Ison in 1898 seemed to give him a new hold on life. Proof that his fame as a Christian thinker was spreading came in 1899 when he crossed the Atlantic to address a great Congregational Assembly in Boston on 'the Evangelical Principle of Authority'.

Of that address J. D. Jones[2] wrote:

In Forsyth's address the Council reached its climax. It was a passionate plea for the Cross as the central thing in our Christian faith. He spoke as a man inspired. He flamed, he burned. . . . We were beyond speech. . . . I wonder whether it was that great afternoon which made us realize here in England what a great gift God had given to our Churches in the person of Peter Taylor Forsyth.

Then in 1901 began the twenty greatest years of Forsyth's life when he accepted an invitation to be principal of Hackney College (now New College), London, which had but recently been recognized as a Divinity School by the University of London. Now for almost two decades, in a life crowded with college work and worries plus the wider demands of

[1] *P.P.M.M.*, 192 f.   [2] *Three Score Years and Ten*, 132.

his own denomination, he poured forth a stream of no less than seventeen books, including all his greatest.

In 1905 he was elected chairman of the Congregational Union of England and Wales and delivered a memorable address on 'the Grace of the Gospel as the Moral Authority in the Church'.

The year 1907 saw Forsyth in Yale for the Lyman Beecher Lectures.

Another and less welcome share of the limelight was his involvement in the controversy created in 1907 by R. J. Campbell's so-called 'New Theology'.

The outbreak of the First World War in 1914 brought deep distress to Forsyth who had so long loved the German people and read their theology. But his own reactions to the crisis were clear and uncompromising. Germany, he held, by deliberately repudiating all moral control when it collided with her commercial interests, had forfeited every right-thinking man's respect. Force, he said, must be met with force for conscience sake, for the world's sake and for the Kingdom's. To leave force to the non-moral would be to leave the world to the tender mercies of the devil.

During these grim years seven books came from his pen, the last of them being the lovely *This Life and the Next* where his ripest thought on the Christian Hope is set down with wonderful simplicity and power.

When the War ended, he was over seventy and desperately tired. Ill health and disease slowly sapped his strength, and at last on the fourth Armistice Day, 11th November 1921, he went to that God whom he had so long and nobly served.

On the memorial panel to him in New College Chapel, where he had often and unforgettably spoken to his students about the deep things of God,[1] there stands the epitaph—and none could be apter—

PER CRUCEM AD LUCEM

II

What did Forsyth look like? Neither tall nor handsome, we are told. His photograph reveals a noble forehead, with large moustache and deep piercing eyes. All his life his health was delicate, so that he once said that from childhood he had never known a day without pain. His was a highly-strung nature which on occasion uttered itself in sharp speech, but there was no abiding malice in it.

If his body was fragile, his mind was extraordinarily quick and, under

[1] See, for example, the valedictory sermon on 'stewards of the mysteries of God', printed at the end of Harry Escott's *P. T. Forsyth, Director of Souls.*

pressure, able to work at almost demonic speed. He had a gay and ready wit, delighting (like Charles Lamb) in puns and *bon mots*. He had a genius for friendship and was very pitiful to the unfortunate. To one such he wrote: 'I am glad you tell me of your depression. I know it well. And how you would be comforted if I could put into your heart the fatherhood it moves in me. . . . In the disheartened hour He is nearer to you than any love of mine could be.'[1]

Above all, as his daughter testifies, he was 'none of your helpless head-in-the-air professors' but, as a friend put it, 'a good man to go hunting tigers with'. Which brings me, by an expressive metaphor, to the other and important side of the man Forsyth on which I should like to dwell a little.

The popular image of a great theologian is of a deep-browed thinker in an ivory tower perpending the mysteries of God remote from the hurly-burly of the workaday world. To this image Forsyth firmly refuses to conform.

As we have seen, in all his pastorates he threw himself heart and soul into the burning issues of the time, ecclesiastical, economic, political. Purely academic scholarship he scorned: he had no patience with a Gospel which appealed only to the West End and never went down into the slums to meet man's sin and despair. He had known the problems of poverty at first-hand in his youth and in the great cities of England; and he took an active interest in the battle being joined between Capitalism and Socialism. Once later he burst out[2]: 'Do not take my arm and lead me away to the dwellings of the pound-a-weeks and the nothing-a-weeks and tell me if I want realities to consider there. I was there, and worked there, and considered there, and have been considering ever since.' In short, for Forsyth, truth—Christian truth—was 'truth in order to be goodness', truth to be tried out in the real world, truth with ineluctable ethical implications for all men. 'We are not saved,' he said, 'if we are saved into neglect of a social salvation.' How could it be otherwise with one who held with Butler that 'morality is the nature of things' and called the Gospel 'God's utmost with man's worst'?

This is no place for a full treatment of Forsyth's view of the Christian Ethic in relation to modern problems. But since we shall mostly be concerned with his theology, we must say something about its social and ethical implications.

There were some in Forsyth's day, as there are still, who take Chris-

---

[1] *W.O.C.* (1946) with Memoir by Jessie Forsyth Andrews, xxv.
[2] *G.O.G.*, 34.

tian Ethics to mean the attempt to apply the principles of Jesus, as summarized in the Sermon on the Mount, to contemporary social and economic problems, and who leave theology out of it as an irrelevance. For example, the Sermon is the thing, and all talk of the Cross represents an illegitimate dragging-in of theology. Forsyth would have none of this. He would have agreed with Brunner that 'Christian Ethics is the science of human conduct as it is determined by Divine conduct'; and if asked to define 'Divine conduct', he would have pointed to the Cross.

The source of Christian Ethic, he said, is the same as the source of Christian life—the merciless mercy of the Cross and God's unspeakable grace disclosed therein. Christian goodness is grace goodness—the goodness that is our response of gratitude to the grace shown in the Atonement. He did not despise the ethical sayings of Jesus—far from it —but he insisted that the power and depth and beauty of these sayings is 'due to their place in the perspective of the supreme and complete Word of Grace which lifts them, fixes and eternalizes them all in the Cross and what was *done* by the Holy there when all saying and showing (even His) were in vain'.[1] Therefore it is the Cross that interprets the Sermon, and not the Sermon the Cross. And all true Christian Ethic— witness St Paul and the other apostolic writers—represents the human action which answers God's grace in the Cross. What we do in responsible Christian action should be really, as it was for St Paul, an abiding expression of gratitude for the Redemption wrought at Calvary:

> Talk they of morals, O Thou dying Lamb?
> The true morality is loving Thee.

In fine, the ethical teachings of Jesus are but illustrations of the spirit that took Christ to Calvary and find their true perspective in that End which crowned all his work on earth. So, he can sum all up thus:

> Love (as the holy and atoning Cross creates love) and do what you
> like. That is Christian Ethic.[2]

This is Forsyth's theory of the Christian Ethic. How and to what lengths did he carry it into practice?

Before we attempt an answer, let us make one point clear. Forsyth declared—and the best New Testament scholarship today supports him —that

[1] *C.E.W.*, v.   [2] Op. cit., 137.

Jesus' ethic is not for the natural man but for the saved, the man lifted from a centre in his own egoism and planted with Christ in God. It is not for the politics of the potsherds of the earth but for the dealings of brothers in the Kingdom of God, not for the nations but for the Church. . . . It is founded on a presupposition of moral regeneration, and cannot come home but in its wake. Such ethic cannot therefore be separated from its context in the Saviour who spoke it, the Kingdom He brought and the power He gave. Nor can it be applied where His power is disowned. It must have its content in the faith that responds, as in the Saviour who spoke. It is an ethic of the Kingdom, and it is for the world only as the world comes to seek first the Kingdom.[1]

Had the Church then no source and warrant for its approach to the wider world beyond the confines of the Church, the world in which capitalists and socialists join issue with each other, the world which is ever troubled by the supreme issue of peace or war?

Of course it had, and for its ethical basis it must, as always, go back to the Cross. The Christian ethic may be summed up as love; but, as the Cross shows, love, if it is to be truly Christian, can never be severed from righteousness which is, as Forsyth said, 'applied holiness'. In fact, the public form of love is righteousness. Once grasp this point, and the Christian attitude to the wider issues, social, economic, political and international, becomes clear. In the realm of industrial relations Christian love will then take the form of a demand for social justice and an insistence that, if the present industrial order stifles the Christian life and rides roughshod over Christian values, the order must be changed. So too in the great issue of peace and war. If the Cross is what it is— God's judgment in Christ crucified on human sin—then the men who identify themselves with Christ, i.e., the Church, have the right to judge sin on a national and international scale (e.g. Germany's in the First World War) and to use force in the name of the Kingdom of God.

In short, for Forsyth Christian Ethics are grounded in the gospel of grace. They are concerned not only with the individual but with society and with nations. But Christianity is not bound up with any particular political or economic system; it must reserve the right to criticize all or any; and, since the Gospel must speak with relevance and power to every such issue, the Church's strategy must be an ever growing and changing thing.

Neo-orthodoxy has sometimes been charged with ethical quietism— witness the famous parody of Barthianism:

[1] *The Expositor*, 1915, 128.

> Sit down, O men of God.
> His Kingdom he will bring,
> Whenever it may please his will.
> You cannot do a thing.

But if Forsyth may be labelled 'neo-orthodox', he was as little open to the charge as Reinhold Niebuhr. In the spirit of the Old Testament prophets but from the vantage point of the Cross, he exercised a truly prophetic ministry through the uneasy calm before the 1914 storm and through all the horrors and heartbreaks of the Kaiser's War. Perhaps this is what his friends meant when they said he was 'a good man to go hunting tigers with'!

III

From Forsyth the man let us turn now to his writings. The first thing to be noted about them is their quantity. In some thirty years he produced no less than twenty-five books (thirteen of them exceeding two hundred pages) plus nearly three hundred articles and contributions to other books.

The next thing to observe is the astonishing diversity of the themes which he handled. We tend to think of him as a writer on the work and person of Christ, on prayer and missions, on Church and sacraments. But besides books on marriage and the Christian ethic of war, he wrote two volumes on art, another on *Socialism, the Church and the Poor*, another on Independency, not to mention studies in the Christian aspect of evolution, Calvinism and Capitalism, the pessimism of Thomas Hardy and Ibsen's treatment of guilt.

The student of Forsyth should of course concentrate on his bigger books, of which we will speak in a moment. But he will miss much of the real Forsyth if he neglects small ones like *The Soul of Prayer* and *This Life and the Next*. And if anyone wants a simple introduction to Forsyth's thought, he could not do better than begin with the Independent Press's reprint, under the omnibus title of *God the Holy Father*, of three long and notable sermons written at the turn of the century— *The Holy Father and the Living Christ*, *Christian Perfection* and *The Taste of Death and the Life of Grace*. These give the key to all his later thinking: here is Forsyth in a nutshell.

Among the major works *Positive Preaching and the Modern Mind*, his Lyman Beecher Lectures at Yale, is probably the best known. It deals not so much with the preacher's craft and homiletics generally as with the gospel, the theology, which should inform all true preaching.

Preaching is seen as truly *sacramental* activity, the prolongation of God's redeeming Act in Christ, and the last chapter is characteristically on 'the moral poignancy of the Cross'.

The longest, most philosophical and most difficult of his books is *The Principle of Authority* (1913). From it you may discover his philosophy of religion, his idea of God, and his theory of the knowledge of God.

The Justification of God, written in 1917 when the First World War was at its grimmest, is a theodicy—a justification of the ways of God in a world where evil manifestly exists and is rampant. It argues that there is no theodicy for the world except in a theology of the Cross. The Cross is God's key to the otherwise undecipherable riddle of history. On that Cross the Son of God died, by his Father's appointing, for the sins of men, so that ever since the powers of evil are in principle judged and doomed. If the holy God did not spare his only Son, we may be sure he will spare no historical convulsion, crisis or calamity needful for the establishment of his sovereignty. This is his most prophetic book and his most timely for us who live in a world threatened with incineration by nuclear holocaust.

But by almost universal consent Forsyth's masterpiece is *The Person and Place of Jesus Christ* (1910). This is his supreme achievement not merely because of its theme, but because in it his style is at its brilliant best, because there are no tantalizing digressions but one long sustained argument that really marches, and because in the last chapters the mystery of the God-man is presented not in the old metaphysical categories of Chalcedon but in moral ones, and the twin concepts of *kenosis* and *plerosis* are invoked, with moving power and skill, to shed light on the union of the human and the divine in the eternal Son of God.

Now a word on the vexed question of Forsyth's style. 'A shower of sky rockets,' said George Jackson. 'Fireworks in a fog,' said Silvester Horne. Those who dislike Forsyth tend to agree. Those who like him talk of his 'vivid and poignant writing'. All agree that *le style c'est l'homme*—it is Forsyth on paper.

We must repudiate the charge of deliberate fog-making, but we cannot deny that Forsyth is often difficult. What makes him so?

His words have something to do with it. Forsyth had the true Celt's feeling for words, so that he often peppered his pages with rare and *recherché* terms that send you to the dictionary for an answer: words like 'fontal' and 'hylic', not to mention polysyllabic wonders like 'plerophory' and 'sequacity'. But it is more than a mere matter of words. The truth is that he had too many ideas in his head all clamouring for expression at the same time.

Moreover, he loved paradox and was ready to argue that in writing theology you could not avoid it. The public, he said, likes to have the obvious thrown in their face, whereupon they immediately turn the other cheek! Paradox is therefore necessary to arrest their attention. Besides, paradox lies at the heart of Christianity—in its dogma of the God-man no less than in the Christian life with its mingling of freedom and dependence (Phil. 2.12 f.).

Yet, admitting all this, we still have not plumbed the depths of the difficulty of his style. J. K. Mozley was surely right when he declared that Forsyth, like St Paul, often found himself straining, even torturing, words and ideas to express the inexpressible. Nor must we forget Harry Escott's explanation of much modern failure to understand Forsyth.[1] It is not just a matter of his words; it is that to many the *experience* of which Forsyth writes—the evangelical experience—is strange. Goethe's couplet sums it up:

> Wer den Dichter will verstehen
> Muss in Dichters Lande gehen.[2]

Nevertheless, when the difficulty of his style has been frankly confessed, it remains true that it often achieves a moving simplicity, that it not seldom puts truth with gnomic and memorable brevity, and that (as any anthology of his writing shows) it is capable of rising to heights of great grandeur.

Here are some of his epigrams and apophthegms:

Half gospels have no dignity and no future. Like the famous mule, they have neither pride of ancestry nor hope of posterity.

Christianity is not the sacrifice we make but the sacrifice we trust.

An undogmatic Christ is the advertisement of a dying faith.

Love's straightening for a tangled world was a cure for its sin—it was propitiation, the mercy of the Cross.

The peace of God is not a glassy calm but a mighty confidence.

The cure of souls must begin at home.

---

[1] This was Forsyth's own explanation of his obscurity. See *P.P.M.M.*, 24; also *G.O.G.*, 45, 'Those who take in earnest an infinite Gospel to such a world, are always obscure to those who do not.'
[2] 'Would you the writer understand,
Then go you must into his land.'

Learn to commit your soul and the building of it to One who can keep it and build it as you never can.

None but the great theologies of redemption are adequate to the great tragedies of the world.

To the gift of epigram he added that of parable and illustration. While his friend Denney confessed that 'an illustration was his despair', Forsyth readily resorted to 'truth embodied in a tale' or the analogy from everyday life. One thinks of the story (in *The Work of Christ*) about the signalman who 'died' (as in a parable) to avert a great railway collision, or of the 'christening mug' so skilfully employed to signify the prevenience of God's grace in baptism.

Yet, when the final defence of Forsyth's style must be made, the lovers of his writing will always point to those supreme passages in his books (and they are not few) where the combination of power and beauty reminds us now of Isaiah, now of Carlyle.

With two such passages we may close this chapter, confident that they will speak for themselves.

The subject of the first is what Pascal called 'the greatness and the misery of man':

We inherit greatness and breathe it. Earth and sky and day and night; stars in the naked heavens, breathings of wind and the coming of spring; hill and plain, rolling tracts, and river and sea; the mist on the long wet moor and above it the black baleful cloud; fleets and camps, cities and realms; valour and power, science, trade, churches, causes, arts, charities; the fidelities of peace and the heroisms of war, the rhythm of order and the stream of progress; the generations that go under and the generations that survive; the energies unseen, the vanished past, the forgotten and unforgettable brave; the majesty of the moral hero and the splendour of the public saint; agonies, love and man's unconquerable mind—Oh, we have a great world, great glories, great records, great prospects and great allies! We inherit greatness and inhabit promise. . . .

But as our sun rises there is a rising cloud. In the moving soul there is a frail seam, an old wound, a tender sore. There is a hollow in the soul's centre, in its last hold no fortress, and in its sanctuary no abiding God. A vanity blights the glory of time, a lameness falls on the strenuous wing, our sinew shrinks at certain touches, and we halt on our thigh; pride falters and the high seems low, and the hour is short, and the candle is out, and what is man that he is accounted of? There is a day of the Lord upon all that is haughty, on lofty tower and tall cedar, and upon all pleasant imagery. And misery, sin and death grow great as all our triumph dwindles on the sight. . . .[1]

[1] *G.H.F.*, 78.

The other concerns a doctrine which meant much to Forsyth and to which we will return—the *kenōsis* of the Son of God, or as he calls it here, 'the emigration of the Divine'.

The height of omnipotence was the power to humble himself, to empty Himself, to go out of Himself and His own bliss. He leaves His native and eternal blessedness and settles in a foreign world. The eternal Father expatriates himself, and in His Son becomes a Pilgrim Father to found a new world. Some speak of the world as due to emanations of the Divine. I would rather speak, if I reverently might, of the emigration of the Divine, of His going forth in His own Person, and not of sending forth His waves. Might I venture on the expression that it was by a Divine emigration and settlement in Christ and His Spirit that earth became a colony of Him and the Church a missionary colony upon the face of the earth? The real idea in the heart of creation was not by almighty magic to make something out of nothing, but it was by moral miracle to make Himself of no account, to become a child and an alien on earth, to suffer and to die. The thousand, the million, the Infinite, becomes a little one; and that is the way in which the little one ever becomes a thousand.[1]

[1] *The Empire for Christ* (1900).

XXI

FORSYTH AND THE BIBLE

DR A. J. GORDON, the American preacher, once related an amusing
conversation he had with the deacon of a church for coloured people.
The deacon could not muster up much enthusiasm for his minister, and,
when pressed to be more explicit, complained that the minister told too
many 'antidotes' in the pulpit. 'But,' returned Dr Gordon, 'I thought
he was a great Bible man.' 'Well,' replied the deacon, 'he's the best man
I ebber seed to take de Bible apart, but he dunno how to put it together
again.'

Forsyth also was 'a great Bible man'. But if he knew all about the
critics' attempts to take the Bible apart, he knew also, as we shall see,
how to put it together again in a way which, when you remember when
he was writing (it was the hey-day of analytical criticism), is little short
of astonishing.

Forsyth did not begin by giving the Bible this central place in his
thinking. To be sure, the scientific criticism of the Bible early engaged
his interest, but for his spiritual stimulus and guidance he resorted
rather to the poets, to Wordsworth, Tennyson, and Browning. But, by
and by, he discovered that, as he put it, 'a curse is on us which these
things cannot lift'. It was then that he turned from the poets to the
apostles, and Mount Calvary, not Mount Parnassus became the dominant peak on his spiritual horizon.

This is how he describes[1] the great change that came over him:

> It pleased God by the revelation of His holiness and grace which the
> great theologians taught me to find in the Bible to bring home to me
> my sin in a way that submerged all the school questions in weight,
> urgency and poignancy.

The great theologians who did him this service were Maurice, Ritschl,
Luther and Calvin. Under their guidance Forsyth began to take the
Bible's way of looking at the great ultimate issues with a new serious-
ness. And, as he read on in them, he found them all pointing him back

---

[1] *P.P.M.M.*, 193.

to the living Word of God in Jesus Christ mediated through what he came to call 'the sacramental Book'.

How did Forsyth regard its authority? To ask this question is to raise the bigger general problem of authority in religion. On this issue Forsyth wrote a great deal. And so deeply did he believe that Protestantism had lost the note of authority and was drifting about 'in a foggy sea of uncharted liberty' that we must spend a few moments discussing the matter.

Where is the seat of religious authority to be found? Three main answers have been given. Roman Catholics have answered in terms of an authoritative Church and a Pope who, when he speaks *ex cathedra*, is infallible. Traditional Protestantism—from *The Westminster Confession* to Billy Graham's 'The Bible says'—has pointed men to an inerrant Bible. And in more recent times many have sought to ground authority in individual religious experience. Forsyth could not rest content with any of these answers. Much as he exalted the idea of the Church, he could not regard it as a continuation of the Incarnation. Christ is sinless; the Church is not. And how could a sinful creation like the Church be a higher authority than the Gospel which called it into being? As for the traditional Protestant answer, criticism had invalidated the old view of the Bible's inerrancy. Nor could Forsyth base authority entirely on so subjective a thing as individual religious experience.

But, in refusing these answers, he also refused to go over to the Liberals with their dilution of the idea of authority and their complete haziness about what the really fundamental thing in Christianity really was. On the contrary, he went back behind both Church and Bible to what created both, the gospel of God's grace to sinners in Christ. Thus he said[1]:

Remember that Christ did not come to bring a Bible but to bring a Gospel. The Bible arose afterwards from the Gospel to serve the Gospel. . . . The Bible, the preacher and the Church are still made by the same thing, the Gospel.

And, be it noted, for Forsyth the Gospel meant pre-eminently God's Act in the Cross, his cure in Christ for the world's moral tragedy, God's revelation of himself breaking in on a sinful race as redemption.

Church, Bible, religious experience—what are they then but channels of a more ultimate authority—the great gospel of God's grace in Christ? Says Forsyth[2]:

[1] *P.P.M.M.*, 15.   [2] *G.O.G.*, 36.

Nothing we experience can secure us on the rock of spiritual reality, or fix us on the last foundation of being, till we experience the Gospel as God's utmost with man's worst.

It is in this gospel of God's grace alone that we possess the moral charter and the moral power which have the *entrée* to man's last recesses and the promises of the ends of the earth.

So we may come back to the question: Wherein does the authority of the Bible reside? Forsyth answers: in its claim (a claim never to be proved to the 'natural' man) to be the record of redemptive revelation. In other words, the authority which rules the Bible is the gospel of God's grace for whose sake the Bible exists. When therefore does the Bible become authoritative for you and me? Answer: when it becomes 'the Sacramental Book'—that is, when, by the Holy Spirit's work, it mediates to us that gospel. Then the old words become luminous with the passage through them of the Holy Ghost, the wire glows with the current, and the soul of the Bible stills and settles us with the grace of God. When this happens, the Bible has done its work, not as a historic document but as a historic means of grace, as a servant of the eternal gospel.

I

Now, with this question of its authority behind us, let us consider Forsyth's general approach to the Bible.

A man who spoke[1] of 'the Holy Spirit's gift of critical scholarship' quite obviously rejected the doctrine of verbal inspiration. But he went further[2]:

Modern scholarship has made of the Bible a new Book. It has in a certain sense rediscovered it. We have, through the labours of more than a century of the finest scholarship in the world, come to understand the Bible in its original sense, as it was never understood before.

Not only so, but he saw clearly the positive value of a sane and moderate Biblical criticism (while castigating the excesses of much German scholarship). Its function, he said,[3] was to 'disengage the kernel from the husk, to save the time so often lost in the defence of outposts, and to discard obsolete weapons and superfluous baggage'. He believed that criticism cleared the ground for the erection of a house of doctrine in which the component materials could be chosen according to their real strength. But if he was no 'fundamentalist', he could go so far as to say[4]:

The true minister ought to find the words and phrases of the Bible so

[1] *C. and S.*, 32.   [2] *W.O.C.*, 36 f.   [3] *P.P.M.M.*, 192.   [4] Ibid., 26.

full of spiritual food and felicity that he has some difficulty in not believing in verbal inspiration.

Next: at a time when analytical criticism of the Bible was almost an obsession of the scholars, Forsyth was already living in what has been called 'the post-critical era'. He had passed from analysis, with all its pains and gains, to synthesis. Listen to this,[1] written in 1905:

> The critical treatment of the Bible must have its place. Let us not make fools of ourselves by denying it. We shall be fighting against God and resisting the Spirit. . . . But its place is secondary, ancillary. It has little place in a pulpit. Criticism is the handmaid of the Gospel, downstairs. The critical study of the Scripture is at its best, and the higher criticism at its highest, when it passes from being merely analytic and becomes synthetic. And the synthetic principle is the Gospel. The analysis of the Bible must serve the history of Grace.

In all the varieties of Biblical religion Forsyth discerned its fundamental unity. What we get in the Bible is Sacramental History—or, as the Germans say, *Heilsgeschichte*—thus:

> The Gospel of Grace in Christ, the purpose and, at last, the act, of Redemption is the key to the Bible. It makes the Bible not a mere chronicle, not a mere set of annals, but history of the greatest kind. . . . In Christ we have the culmination of the long revealing line of Old Testament prophecy. We have in a whole permanent personality what the prophets had in their fleeting vision and burthen. We have God seeking, and finding, and saving us. God tells us through man's word, or by his own deeds, the secret of His purpose, His deep decrees and universal will. It is a purpose, will and work of grace, of love, of Redemption, of Salvation. To carry home this is the object of the Bible. For this the Bible exists. From this the Bible sprang.[2]

The Bible's unity, then, is a dramatic unity of action—a unity issuing in a great historic crescendo—the coming of God's Kingdom in Christ. Need I say that this is the only proper *Christian* way of regarding the Bible, for the simple and sovereign reason that it was the Lord's way? For evidence we need only read the parable of the Wicked Vinedressers or Luke 11.49 f. But Forsyth has amplified[3] the point for us:

> Christ used the Bible as a means of grace, not as a manual of Hebrew or other history. . . . He found in it the long purpose and deep scope of God's salvation. He cared for events only as they yielded his Father's grace. . . . What he saw was the whole movement of Old Testament history rather than its pragmatic detail. He cared little for

---

[1] *Contemporary Review*, Oct. 1905, 579.
[2] Ibid., 576.   [3] Ibid., 585 f.

what our scholars expound—the history of Israel. What he found in the Old Testament was not the prophets' thoughts of God but God's action in Israel by prophet, priest or king, God's invasion of them and their race by words and deeds of gracious power.... *The torch he carried through the Old Testament was the Gospel of Grace....* He read it with the eyes of faith, not of science. And he read it as a whole.

The Bible, therefore, for Forsyth, is the record of the unique self-disclosure of the living and gracious God in the stuff of human history. And when Forsyth talked about Revelation, he took the word seriously and construed it in the best modern way. The 'propositional view'—that Revelation is communicated in a series of statements or inspired truths—he dismissed as 'the bad old way'. 'Do we not yet understand,' he exclaimed,[1] 'that the true nature of Revelation is that it should come by historic facts and deeds rather than by truths?' Revelation is redemptive, not propositional. It is not the conveyance of truth about God and his action; it is God's actual coming and acting. Above all, it is the holy love of God dealing with the sin and guilt of man, once and for all, in 'the hell-harrowing and heaven-scaling Cross of Christ'. The burning focus of Revelation is 'the merciless mercy of the Cross and the Son unspared for us'.

II

As we turn to the New Testament, where Forsyth's chief interest lay, let us remember that he was writing, roughly, between the beginning of the Boer War and the end of the First World War. (Let me also remind you that *Dogmatikers* are commonly accused of lagging about twenty years behind the *Neutestamentlers*.) In the light of this, Forsyth's penetration and prescience are nothing short of remarkable. Let us take three examples, one touching the nature of religion, the second the nature of the Gospels, and the third that of apostolic inspiration.

Take first 'the idea of the Holy'. One of the most notable books published between the two World Wars was Otto's book of that title. In it he argued that the essence of religion lay not in knowledge or in conduct but in awe—in the sense of the utter holiness of God. But long before this Forsyth had discovered that 'the knowledge of the holy is understanding' (Prov. 9.10) and in book after book insisted that holiness (not heartiness) was the character of God, as the revelation in Christ was one not of love but of *holy* love.

The early 'nineteen-twenties' saw the rise in Germany of the Form Critics, Bultmann, Dibelius, Schmidt and the rest. One axiom of this

[1] *P.P.J.C.*, 119.

new set of critics was that the Gospels were written 'from faith to faith'; that, so far from being biographies, they reflect the religious faith and convictions of the communities in which they originated. But away back in 1905 Forsyth's readers were being told how wrong it was to regard the Gospels as the 'Boswellizing' of a great Figure and that 'the object of the New Testament writers was not to provide biographical material but evangelical testimony'. The Gospels are 'pamphlets in the service of the Church—to assist the Gospel'. 'They are engrossed with Christ, not as a fascinating character but as the Gospel to us of the active grace of God': 'The evangelist with his narrative was but an acolyte of the apostle with his Gospel.'[1]

For a final example: in 1918 Barth startled the theological world by his exegesis of the Epistle to the Romans, in which he took a new and high view of apostolic inspiration. The letters of the apostles were true vehicles of revelation because their subject matter was the Spirit of Christ, and in them that Spirit spoke his saving truth through chosen and commissioned witnesses. But years before Forsyth had been saying the same thing: the apostolic witness to Christ is the authentic teaching of the risen Christ, given through the Holy Spirit. What we have in the apostles' letters, he said, is 'Christ explaining Himself, the Saviour still preaching His salvation, not only unsilenced by death but in the fulness achieved by its conquest'.[2]

These and other trends were to bring a new depth to New Testament studies resulting in a revival of Biblical theology. In this country the change came in the late nineteen-twenties and was first clearly seen in the writing of Sir Edwyn Hoskyns. What we are now realizing is that Forsyth, though not primarily a New Testament scholar, had penetrated to as great a depth as Hoskyns in his New Testament studies.

III

To illustrate this point, we cannot do better than begin with the problem of the nature of the apostolic Gospel.

When I began serious study of theology, the scholars were still talking tirelessly about 'Paulinism'. There were few to tell me that, basically, Paul's gospel was that of the other apostles. On the contrary, it was common opinion that, vis-à-vis the other apostles, Paul and his gospel were in a minority of one. Not till 1936 was this delusion exploded. In that year C. H. Dodd's *Apostolic Preaching* showed conclusively that 'in the beginning was the *kerygma*', that long before the written Gospels

[1] *P.P.J.C.*, 12; *Contemporary Review*, Oct. 1905, 581.   [2] *P.O.A.*, 134.

appeared—before even Paul began writing—there was a common apostolic Gospel—a *kerygma* shared by all the apostles—whose outline could be reconstructed.

Let me not say a word in dispraise of Dodd. But was he really the first to discover the *kerygma*? Here are some sentences written before the First World War[1]:

> In the matter of the vital creative meaning of Christ's person and death, Peter, Paul and John were all of one mind. . . . There was of course no universal theological formula, there was not an orthodoxy; but certainly there was a common apostolic Gospel, a *kerygma*. . . . And this theological *kerygma* stands for us as the common chord in the three great names who represent the apostolate.

Forsyth was writing a quarter of a century before Dodd.

IV

Now let us turn to the Synoptic Gospels. Nowadays most scholars would agree that the dominant theme of the first three Gospels is the Kingdom of God, eschatologically interpreted, and that the phrase 'realized eschatology', however inadequate, contains a real core of truth.

In Forsyth's day it was far otherwise. When Liberal evangelicals spoke then of the Kingdom of God, they meant some kind of Christian commonwealth and they interpreted its coming in terms of social evolution, 'first, the blade, then the ear, then the full corn in the ear'. ('What is that', asked Henry Drummond, 'but evolution?') But, as we now know, the Kingdom of God in the Gospels is not so much an evolving as an invading, not so much a process as a crisis. It is the living God actively exercising his saving sovereignty in human affairs for men's salvation. So Otto, Dodd and others have taught us in our day.

But, years ago, Forsyth showed that he was 'not far from the Kingdom of God':

'The Kingdom of God,' he wrote,[2] 'is the emergence into the life of history, both by growth and crisis, of that saving Sovereignty which is the moral power and order of the spiritual world.' And he was just as sure as our 'realized eschatologists' that the Kingdom in the Gospels is not just a shining hope on the far horizon of history but, in a real sense, a blessed *fait accompli* (Luke 10.23 f. Q). 'The Cross of Christ,' he said,[3] 'is not just the preliminary of the Kingdom; it is the Kingdom breaking in.' And again: 'The more you insist that a soul can be saved,

---

[1] *P.O.A.*, 126 f.; see also the *Contemporary Review*, Oct. 1905, 582 f.
[2] *T.L.T.N.*, 60.   [3] *J.O.G.*, 77.

and personality secured, by Christ's finished work, the more you must contend that the Kingdom is not merely coming but is come, and is active in the Spirit among us.'[1]

It would be foolish to claim that Forsyth had all the right answers to the questions we ask about the Kingdom. (When he calls the Church 'the Kingdom in the making', some of us would demur, and it must be admitted that he did less than justice to the *future* aspects of the Kingdom and the New Testament hope of the Parousia.) Yet he had grasped the profound truth contained in Origen's word *autobasileia*—had discerned that the person of Christ is indissolubly bound up with the Kingdom, that Christ *is*, in a real sense, the Kingdom. This comes out with clarity in his answer to the question why, if the preaching of the Kingdom dominates the Synoptics, it would seem to be on its way out in Acts and in Paul is almost replaced by the preaching of Christ. 'The Gospel of Christ,' replies Forsyth,[2] 'replaced the Gospel of the Kingdom because He became all that the Kingdom contained. . . . Like "Messiah", the Kingdom was an Old Testament phrase which served to enclose what He brought in Himself; and the pitcher, the phrase, was broken as the light shone. . . . The Kingdom was great with Him. The Gospel of the Kingdom was Christ in essence; Christ was the Gospel of the Kingdom in power. The Kingdom was Christ in a mystery; Christ was the publication, the establishment of the Kingdom. . . . He was the truth of His own greatest Gospel. It is wherever He is. To have him is to ensure it.'

From the Kingdom turn now to the problem of interpreting the parables.

At the end of last century Jülicher sounded the death-knell of that arbitrary allegorizing of the parables which had bedevilled their interpretation from the sub-apostolic age. The gist of what he had to say was this. The parables of Jesus are similitudes, not allegories. Therefore, in studying a parable, concentrate on the one *tertium comparationis*, or point of likeness, for the sake of which the parable is told, and regard all the rest as dramatic machinery necessary for the telling of the tale.

That Forsyth has mastered Jülicher's lesson, this quotation will show:

What is the function of a parable? It is one of the great discoveries and lessons taught us by modern scholarship that parables are not allegories, because they exist for the sake of one central idea. While we may allow ourselves, under the suggestion of the Holy Spirit, to receive hints of edifying truth from this or the other phrase or detail

of the parable, we have chiefly to ask: What was in the mind of Christ
for the sake of which He uttered the parable? Each parable puts in an
ample ambit one central idea. Now the one ruling idea in the parable
of the Prodigal Son is the idea of the centrality, the completeness, the
unreservedness, fullness, wholeheartedness of God's grace—the absolute fullness of it, rather than the method of its action.[1]

(This in reply to those who wanted to find the whole Gospel in
the parable.)

Throughout his writings you will find examples of Forsyth's insight
into the meaning of the parables as Christ uttered them. But even more
important than the meaning of the parables is the whole interpretation
of the Story of Jesus in the Gospels. When Forsyth was writing, men
were still trying to squeeze Jesus into the moulds of human psychology,
or to place him in the succession of spiritual genius. The result was to
reduce him to a figure which, as he saw, could no longer do the work of
Jesus. It was Schweitzer who first taught us that we cannot tell the
Story of Jesus without a theology; and Forsyth was swift to take the
point. Only a *theological* Christ, i.e. a Christ whose leading motives were
theological, could make sense of the Story told in the Gospels or 'the
thing he was to accomplish for God at Jerusalem when he flung himself
on the Cross'. Jesus, in fact, broke his nation on a theology. He knew
his death 'would throw his people in the wrong'. This was the heart of
his agony. Their greatest Lover was to be their final doom. But nothing
turned him from it, because he knew it was God's way. And so 'amid
the judgment' he offered his obedience to God for his Kingdom and
made the sacrifice required by the holiness of that Will. Here is how
Forsyth explains Christ's grief over Jerusalem and the Crisis of the
Cross:

> It was the agony of an old nation not only dying but damned; and all
> its vast tragedy transpiring not only within the soul of one Man but
> (chief horror!) by the solemn choice and awful act of that one Man
> himself, and He its lover. Think of a whole nation proud, stubborn
> and passionate, with an ingrained belief in a world prerogative and
> mission, expiring in one Man, in whom also by a dreadful collision
> was rising the Kingdom of God they had forsworn; and the fate of
> God's whole Kingdom in the world decided in an Armageddon of that
> one spirit; a world's eternal warfare and destiny forced through the
> channel of one soul vast enough, whatever He did not know or could
> not do, to be in His death alive and adequate to such an issue.[2]

Nothing could better show how Forsyth was able to read *in depth* the
story of Jesus and his Cross.

[1] *W.O.C.*, 106.   [2] *The Expositor*, July 1915.

V

Now, to the Apostle.

Tirelessly and perseverantly Forsyth kept driving men back to St Paul as the supreme interpreter of Christ. This was not a popular line to take in days when men tended to write off the apostle as the gratuitous sophisticator of the Gospel. Forsyth strongly demurred. St Paul he named 'the Fifth Evangelist', declaring that there was 'more inspiration in a creative Paul than in a compiling evangelist'.[1] Not only was Paul's Gospel fundamentally the same as that of the other apostles, but (as he put it[2]) 'Christ taught Paul in the Spirit as truly as He taught the disciples in the flesh.' His thesis[3] was that 'God's Son Jesus needed prophets, as God's Son Israel needed prophets, to expound His divine meaning and purpose'; and founding on I Corinthians 2 (especially verse 16: 'we have the mind of Christ' means 'we have the theology of Christ') he explained apostolic inspiration thus[4]:

> The apostolic documents are the prolongation of the message of Jesus They are Christ himself interpreting his finished work through men in whom not they lived but He lived in them. Christ in the apostles interpreted his finished work as truly as in his life-time He interpreted His unfinished work.

The value of this view is clear. If, for example, the centrality of the Cross in Paul depends not on individual and subjective opinion but on the inspiration of Christ himself, the theology of men like Forsyth carries Dominical authority. At any rate, a man who takes this view will obviously have a quick and instinctive sympathy with St Paul's mind.

'God forbid that I should glory save in the Cross of our Lord Jesus Christ,' said St Paul. And so did Forsyth in all his writings. You might even call him a man of one idea—the atoning Cross. But that idea—or, rather, act—was for him something universal, cosmic, eternal. In the Cross he saw the centre of history and of the moral universe, and he was always summoning his readers to adjust their compasses by 'the inexhaustible Cross'. In the next chapter we shall have to wrestle with his doctrine of the Atonement, and we shall see how much it owes to great passages in Paul like II Cor. 5.14-21. Suffice it now to say with J. K. Mozley[5]:

---

[1] *Contemporary Review*, Oct. 1905, 584.   [2] *G.H.F.*, 18.
[3] *Contemporary Review*, Oct. 1905, 581.
[4] *P.P.J.C.*, 60. *Nous* in I Cor. 2.16 means 'teaching'. 'Our thoughts are the thoughts of Christ' (Moffatt).
[5] In *Church and Sacraments* (new edition), viii.

Forsyth goes round and round like a thunderstorm, but again and again he returns back on his tracks as though he could not bear to be out of sight of the lights of home, the home that Christ made for men by his Cross, the home which in a very real sense for Forsyth was the Cross.

'The life that I now live in the flesh,' said St Paul, 'I live by faith in the Son of God who loved me and gave himself for me.' Faith here is man's life-response to the grace of God in the Cross. Just as Forsyth, like Paul, made the Cross central, so his concept of faith corresponded to the apostle's. We remember how in Romans 4 Paul singles out Abraham as a pattern of the true man of faith, the man who, when God spoke to him, took God at his word and obeyed. Just so Forsyth said: 'Faith is taking God at His Word—at His living Word, Christ—His urgent, reticent, gracious, masterful Word, Christ.'[1] And again: 'Faith is the grand venture in which we commit our whole soul and future to the confidence that Christ is not an illusion but the reality of God.'[2] And as the apostle spoke of 'faith working through love' (Gal. 5.6), Forsyth could write: 'The good live by faith and work by love—charity is the rose-bloom of Christian faith.'[3]

The great Pauline phrase 'in Christ' is yet another instance of his insight. Since Deissmann's monograph in 1892 its meaning has been much debated. At first scholars held that it described the believer's intimate personal fellowship with his living Lord. They were not wrong but they had grasped only half of the truth. Then Schweitzer and others taught us to hear the strong *corporate* overtones in the formula, and we began to see that to be 'in Christ' very often meant to be a member of Christ's community, the Church. But this was no news to Forsyth. 'The same act which sets us "in Christ",' he wrote,[4] 'sets us also in the society of Christ.' 'To be a Christian is not to attach one's salvation to a grand individual, but it is to enter Christ, and to enter Christ is in the same act to enter the Church which is in Christ. Faith in Christ is faith in One whose indwelling makes a Church, and who carries a Church within His corporate person.'[5]

The reference to the corporate Christ suggests a final example of Forsyth's fidelity to the New Testament.

When the New Testament writers refer to the work of Christ, they generally do it in a *racial* way. For them, salvation is far more than the nexus of the individual, *qua* individual, with the Saviour. As our Lord

[1] *G.H.F.*, 18.   [2] *P.P.J.C.*, 205.   [3] *C. and S.*, 25, 18.
[4] Op. cit., 61.   [5] Op. cit., 43.

had declared that he was giving his life to ransom 'all men' (Mark 10.45), so Paul and John never tire of saying that his death was a death for the whole human race (see Rom. 5; II Cor. 5; John 1.29; 11.52; I John 2.2, etc.). This racial note was not congenial to much Protestant thinking which tended to preach 'an individualist salvation by private bargain'. Here again, Forsyth, if he did not march with the *Zeitgeist*, was in step with the New Testament. Like St Paul he always envisaged the individual soul in a universal salvation. He said: 'It took a world's salvation to save me'; and—

> Christ was in his victory the Agent of the race. . . . He was no mere lone individual. . . . If He overcame the world, it was humanity that won. If Christ died for all, all died in the Act. We rise because He rose, and we rise not like Him but in Him.[1]

VI

Now, leaving St Paul, let us take three general topics of New Testament theology: the Church, preaching, and Christian perfection.

During the last thirty years scholars have been re-discovering the true New Testament meaning of *ecclēsia*. In the LXX the word normally translates *qahal*, the usual Hebrew term for the gathered People of God. So, when the first followers of Christ called themselves the *ecclēsia theou*, they were claiming to be the true People of God, at once old and new. If we read of local congregations called *ecclēsiai*, these are not discrete churches but outcrops of the one Great Church. So K. L. Schmidt writes[2]: 'The fact that a number of local communities grew together gradually as an organization creates the impression of a development from separate local churches to one universal Church. But this impression is misleading. The important fact is that the local congregation was conscious of itself as the representative of the universal Church.'

But Forsyth had already taken the point[3]: 'What the apostles planted,' he said, 'was not churches but stations of the Church. What the Gospel created was not a crowd of churches but the one Church in various places. What we have everywhere is the one Church of Christ put down here and there, looking out in Corinth, Ephesus or Thessalonica.'

Or consider the nature of true preaching. Examine our best modern authorities, and you find them agreeing that *praedicatio Verbi Divini est Verbum Divinum*. Preaching is a part of God's saving activity, the

---

[1] *J.O.G.*, 220.   [2] *The Church* (Bible Key Words), 69.
[3] *C. and S.*, 68.

Gospel. In it the event recurs, God's salvation in Christ continues, the Gospel reverberates. Then we turn up Forsyth, writing in 1907,[1] to find this:

> Preaching is the Gospel prolonging and declaring itself. The gift of God's grace was, and is, His work of Gospel. And it is this Act which is prolonged in the word of the preacher and not merely declared.

The truth of course is that this doctrine of preaching is as old as one who called the gospel 'the power of God unto salvation'. 'We come as Christ's ambassadors,' he says (II Cor. 5.20). Here saving act and saving message are inseparable, as the parallel clauses show: 'who reconciled us to himself through Christ, and gave us the work of reconciliation'. (Cf. *synergountes* in 6.1: 'sharing in God's work'.) Preaching is conceived as a real part of the saving event, no mere commentary on it; and the message, as Bornkamm[2] says, 'derives its authority from the fact that Christ himself speaks in his ambassador's work or—what is the same thing for Paul—God himself makes his appeal in using the apostle as his mouthpiece'.

From preaching turn now to the New Testament idea of perfection. The great mistake here—a mistake made, according to Forsyth, by both Roman Catholics and pietists—has been to equate perfection with sinlessness. But this is not, he declares, the prevailing New Testament view. There perfection is not the complete achievement of Christian character, but the right relation to God in Christ, which is a matter of faith.

So 'the saints in the New Testament are not the saintly but the believing. What Christ demanded of those who came to him was not character, not achievement, but faith, faith in himself as God's grace. That was the one demand of God, and to answer it is perfection. . . . The man of faith is perfect before God because his will is in the relation to God which is God's will for him, and he has the germ and the conditions which will work out in sanctifying time to ethical perfection as well.'[3]

Enough has been said to suggest Forsyth's view of the Bible and to show in particular how profound an interpreter of the New Testament he was. This is undoubtedly a prime secret of his greatness as a systematic theologian.

Though it is a truism, it perhaps needs saying that all true Christian doctrine must be built upon the person and work of Christ as they are

---

[1] *P.P.M.M.*, 3.   [2] In Kittel's *TWNT* VI, 682.   [3] *G.H.F.*, 126.

exhibited to us in the pages of the New Testament. This means that theologians must base their doctrine of Christ upon the most faithful portrait that objective Biblical scholarship can paint from the data preserved in the Gospels. But it means more, as Forsyth saw. 'It takes the whole of the New Testament to show who Christ is.' To the evidence of the Gospels we must always add that of the apostolic men—of Paul, John, Peter and the rest—if we are to appraise the Fact of Christ in its full and true significance. (Otherwise, in adding 'the apostle' to 'the Gospel', the makers of the New Testament Canon stand convicted of grave error.)

This is what Forsyth so superbly did in all his writing, not forgetting to invoke also the testimony of the Church's experience down the centuries. But experience, valuable as it is, is not by itself enough. We must ever keep returning to ponder anew, and in depth, the Word that God spoke to our world in Christ and him crucified, of which the Bible is the unique record. Nay, more than record; for, as Forsyth insisted, it is 'the Sacramental Book'. We have, he said, but one great Sacrament —that of God's redeeming grace in Christ's Cross. In this sacrament the Bible takes the place of the elements; and it can mediate the historic grace of God no less than they. This is why, by the Holy Spirit's power, the ancient words can still speak contemporaneously and become to us the very Word from the Beyond for our human predicament today. And, to round off this chapter, I cannot do better than set before you, in his own words, a magnificent example of what Forsyth means[1]:

I read the story of the father who beseeches Christ to heal his son. I hear the answer of the Lord, 'I will come down and heal him.' 'Him!' That means me. The words are life to my distempered soul. I care little for them (when I need them most) as a historic incident of the long past, an element in the discussion of miracles. They do not serve their divinest purpose till they come to me as they came to that father. They come with a promise here and now. I see the heavens open and the Redeemer at the right hand of God. I hear a great voice from heaven, and these words are the words of the Saviour himself to me, 'I will come down and heal him.' And upon them he rises from his eternal throne, He takes his way through a ready lane of angels, arch-angels, the high heavenly host, and the glorious fellowship of saints. They part at His coming, for they know where He would go. These congenial souls do not keep Him, and these native scenes do not detain Him. But on the wings of that word he moves from the midst of complete obedience, spiritual love, holy intelligence, ceaseless worship and eternal praise. He is restless amid all that in search of me—

[1] *G.O.G.*, 66 f.

me sick, falling, lost, despicable, desperate. He comes, He finds, He heals me, on the wings of these words. I do not ask the critics for assurance that the incident took place exactly as recorded. I will talk of that when I am healed. It is a question for those who are trying to frame a biography of Jesus, or discussing the matter of miracles. It has brought to dying me the life of Christ. . . . For me the words are more than historical, they are sacramental. They carry not a historic incident merely, but a historic Gospel. Historically, they were never said to me. I was not in the thought of Jesus when He spoke them; neither was I in his thought upon the Cross. But by the witness of the Spirit to my faith they come as if they were said to no one else. I was in His Gospel. They come to me as they are in God. And I live on them for long. . . . And I wait by their hope, and in the strength of their life I go many nights and days till I come to another mount of God.

XXII

FORSYTH'S THEOLOGY

In this chapter, greatly daring, we are going to range rapidly over the whole field of Forsyth's theology. The treatment is bound to be summary; but if it provides a broad picture, it will have served its purpose.

We begin with the question: What was Forsyth's aim in all his theologizing?

It was certainly not to emulate R. J. Campbell by providing a 'New Theology'. We stand in trust, he said, of the final revelation, 'and whatever new thing awaits us must be a fresh ray from the old faith, and a fresh shoot from the old creed'.[1] Listen to him speaking as the Chairman of the Congregational Union:

> The old orthodoxies can never again be what they were; but one thing in them draws me and sustains me amidst much that is hopelessly out of date. And it is this, that they had a true eye for what really mattered in Christianity, and especially that they did grapple with the final facts in human nature, the abysses of moral experience, the wickedness of the human heart, and its darling self-will. They closed with ultimates. They did not heal lightly the wound of the people. . . . It is the grace of Israel we need; for the grace of Greece fails heart, and flesh, and moral will. It is subjective sand when we want objective rock. It does not enable us to keep our feet. We need a hand to lift us by the hair, if need be, and hurt us much in the doing of it, if only it sets us on the Rock of Ages. And the old Puritans (now sixpence a volume octavo) at least do that. And they do it because, with a very criticizable theology, they stood at the centre of things with their religion of the moral Atonement, of a free but most costly Gospel. They grasped what makes God the Christian God—not only a free grace but a costly. It is not only the freedom of His grace but its infinite price to Him that makes God God. 'By terrible things in righteousness dost Thou answer us, O God of our salvation.'[2]

What Forsyth aimed to give his generation was not a new theology but a renovated one—an orthodoxy modernized, moralized, revitalized.

Second: Forsyth was no system-maker. To the Tennysonian rule that

> Our little systems have their day,
> They have their day and cease to be

[1] *C.E.W.*, 127. [2] *G.O.G.*, 61 f.

systematic theologies which aspire to comprehend the whole counsel of God to men in Christ, are no exception. Forsyth went further. He said that finality was in God and his Act, and that with a final system we should have no God.

Yet if he is no system-maker, his writing is wonderfully unified by the presence in it of a few dominant ideas so that, in the result, not many writers have fewer loose ends to their thought than Forsyth.

Where then do we start? With Forsyth there is only one right place to begin—at the Cross.

I

The Cross, for Forsyth, was the diamond pivot on which his whole scheme of Christian truth revolved. How then did he conceive the work of Christ?

To begin with, he did not try to refurbish any historic form of the doctrine. On the contrary, he rejected this or that view held by the doctors of the Church. We must never think, he said, of grace as procured by the Atonement. We must not say that Christ offered an equivalent suffering for our punishment. We must not speak of a transfer of guilt as if it were a 'ledger amount which could be shifted by Divine finance'.

But these negatives do not carry us very far. Let us therefore, as we approach his positive teaching, note two things:

First, if there is one New Testament passage which more than any other sheds light for him on Christ's work, it is II Cor. 5.14-21. Here it is described as 'reconciliation' which in turn rests on 'atonement', since 'God was in Christ reconciling the world to himself' is immediately followed by 'not counting their trespasses' and 'God made him to be sin for us who knew no sin'. (Note: 'Atonement' is the covering of sin by something which God himself provided, and therefore the covering of sin by God himself; whereas 'Reconciliation' denotes the total result of Christ's work in permanently changing the relation between God and man from hostility to peace.)

Second, we shall never begin to understand Forsyth unless we take God's holiness as seriously as he did.

The nature of God, he kept saying, is not love but *holy* love. Why this accent on the adjective? Because his contemporaries, reacting too far from their forefathers' picture of God as 'the Lord Chief Justice of the world', had so sentimentalized the love of God as to lose touch with the Bible (where 'Our Father' is immediately followed by 'Hallowed be thy

L

name') and to turn the problem of Divine forgiveness into a matter of easy indulgence, on the principle of Heine's 'God will forgive me. That is his business.' But, said Forsyth, the essence of God's love is its awful purity; it cannot traffic with the unholy; it must deal exigently with sin. If we are to think of God aright, we must think of him as the Holy Father who loves all his creatures with a seeking, self-bestowing love; but it is a love which, though it desires nothing but the responsive love of his children, is inexorable against evil—whose obverse side is indeed wrath. With human sin this Holy Father can make no terms; and the whole moral crisis of things comes to a head in the opposition between God's holiness and the world's unholiness, the guilt of sinful men.

Now it is plain that we cannot ourselves atone or reconcile. (If we could, we should be, as Luther said, 'the proudest jackasses under heaven'.) What is needed to put things right is an act of reparation to God's holiness which will alter the whole relation between God and man and repair their broken fellowship—an Act of God himself, in fact, the Act of the Cross.

Forsyth sums it up thus[1]:

> The Holy Father's first care is holiness. The first charge on a Redeemer is satisfaction to that holiness. The Holy Father is one who does and must atone . . . as Holy Father He offers a sacrifice rent from His own heart. It is made to Him by no third party, but by Himself in His Son, and it is made to no foreign power but to His own holy nature and law.

Forsyth, then, held an objective doctrine of the Atonement; but he saw Christ's work in its *double* character—as an Act of God and as an act done in humanity. If he stressed the first more than the second, he only did what Scripture does. Moreover, by so doing, he avoided two fatal errors:

(1) the view which regards the Atonement as the appeasement of an angry God by a loving Christ;
(2) the destruction of the moral unity of the Godhead.

Accordingly, while he can speak of Christ's dealing with the Father, in his atoning work, he speaks mostly of this work as one that only God can do.

Christ's dealing with the Father (to take it first) was, like an iceberg, largely hidden. 'The great thing was done with God. It was independent of our knowledge of it. The greatest thing ever done in the world was

[1] *G.H.F.*, 4.

done out of it. The most ever done for us was done behind our backs. ... Doing this *for* us was the first condition of doing anything *with* us.'[1]

Of the Atonement as an Act of God he writes[2]:

Atonement is an Old Testament phrase, where the idea is that of the covering of sin from God's sight. But by whom? Who was skilful enough to hoodwink the Almighty? Who covered the sin? The all-seeing God alone. ... Atonement means the covering of sin by something which God had himself provided and therefore the covering of sin by God Himself.

And again[3]:

The real objectivity of the Atonement is not that it was made to God, but by God. ... The real objective element is therefore that God made it and gave it finished to man, not that it was made to God by man.

We may now ask: What, for Forsyth, were the main elements in Christ's atoning work?

J. K. Mozley answers[4]: 'The Cross is God's saving Act in Christ by virtue of two moral elements which go to make up its total value. The first is expressed by the words "sacrifice" and "obedience", the second by the words "confession" and "judgment".'

Let us take the pairs of words in turn.

Whether in the Old Testament or the New, obedience is the truth of sacrifice. In the work God gave Christ to do—the sacrificial shedding of his blood—Christ made a complete sacrifice of his will—that will which 'is our ownest own, the only and dear thing we can and ought really to sacrifice'.[5] And the satisfying thing to the Holy Father was not an equivalent penalty—as if he were a great Shylock demanding his pound of flesh—but Christ's obedient sanctity. For in Christ's sufferings the atoning thing was not their amount but their obedience.

Now consider the element of judgment and confession. Because God is holy, he must judge men's sins, and the Cross shows him doing this. 'Him who knew no sin.' says St Paul, 'God made to be sin for us.' Christ experienced sin as God does, while he experienced its effects as man does. 'There is a penalty and curse for sin, and Christ consented to enter that region.'[6] (We think of the Agony in the Garden and of the Cry of Dereliction—that dereliction which, according to Forsyth, was the real 'Descent into Hell'.) 'God did not punish Christ,' declares[7]

[1] Op. cit., 19.   [2] *W.O.C.*, 54 f.   [3] Op. cit., 92 f.
[4] *The Doctrine of the Atonement*, 184.   [5] *The Cruciality of the Cross*, 192.
[6] *W.O.C.*, 147.   [7] *P.P.M.M.*, 248.

Forsyth, 'but Christ entered the dark shadow of God's penalty upon sin.'

But his role was not merely passive. From within the sphere of sin's penalty he actively confessed God's holiness. Nor did he do it with his lips alone but 'in a far more mighty way, by act and deed of life and death'. He did justice to God's holiness by confessing it, while under sin's judgment, with a holiness equal to the Father's own. And it was this confession which established his Father's holiness, making possible the forgiveness of the world which could only be achieved by its judgment.

How does this affect us? Directly and deeply, because in it Christ acted as our Representative. Yet not by the will of man choosing Christ, but by the will of Christ choosing man and freely identifying himself with him. So, from the midst of the fires of judgment, there came from Christ, on our behalf, a solidary confession of God's holiness.

What then is the fruit of the Atonement? Nothing less than a world's reconciliation. What Christ saved was the human race, and we are each of us saved in a social salvation. But is the world's reconciliation really accomplished, without the race of men all repenting and putting their faith in Christ? Yes, in principle. The thing is done; it is not to do. What remains is to follow it up, actualize it, appropriate it.

Thus we reach a very important element in Forsyth's doctrine. Our holiness, he says, was latent in Christ's holiness which alone could and must create it. Christ is the pledge not only of God's love to us but also of our response to it by a total change of will and life. And Forsyth sees the prolongation of Christ's work in the New Humanity he creates. 'When you think of what Christ did for the race,' he observes, 'never forget our living union with Him.' Think then of that summary reconciliation of Christ's being worked out to cover the whole of history and to enter each soul by the Spirit. 'Christ stretches a hand through time,' he writes,[1] 'and seizes the far-off interest of our tears. . . . All His holiness is not only fair and beloved of God, but it is also great with the penitence of the race He sanctifies.' 'Christ, in his victorious death and risen life, has power to unite the race to Himself, and to work His complete holiness into its actual experience and history.'[2] Before us rises the picture of a Christ presenting along with his own obedience the penitent love he is yet to create in his People, and of the Holy Father accepting not only him but us in him and with him. We are left with the vision of a God whose mercy is as his majesty, and whose

[1] *W.O.C.*, 193.   [2] Op. cit., 130.

omnipotence is shown chiefly in forgiving, redeeming and settling all souls in worship in the temple of a new heaven and a new earth full of holiness.

Which brings us to Forsyth's last point—the cosmic eschatology of the Cross. This theme he developed in his 'theodicy', *The Justification of God*, during all the horrors of the First World War. The Cross (he argues) is the once-for-all vindication in history of God's righteousness and the pledge of the perfect consummation of his holy purpose. To the eye of faith, God appears as subduing history and all its evils to the pattern of reconciliation shown at Calvary. 'If God's holy way,' he writes,[1] 'spared not His own Son, i.e. His own self, that holiness is secured finally for the whole world with its most cynical immorality, deadly malignity, and cruel frightfulness. . . . If the greatest act in the world, and the greatest crime there, became, by the moral, the holy victory of the Son of God, the source not only of endless blessing to man, but of perfect satisfaction and delight to holy God, then there is no crime, not even this war, that is outside His control or impossible for His purpose.' In short, the God of the Cross has the evil of the world, even such a world as we see, in the hollow of his hand, and we may believe in his final and complete victory over it.

Criticize this doctrine of Forsyth's as we will,[2] we cannot deny its depth, its richness, its grandeur. Here he shows us the Son's dealing with the Father for us, which is also the Father's own dealing in judgment and grace with the problem of man's sin and salvation. He shows us also how the work of Christ provides the grand reconciliation between God and man—at once a finished work and an inheritance to be appropriated by the faith and penitence of later generations. And he shows us how this work is not only the source of a world-wide salvation but the vindication of God's own righteousness and the pledge of his ultimate victory.

Once (in a source which I cannot trace) Forsyth told a parable which, if it does not cover all the facets of his doctrine, catches the spirit of it, and may fitly sum it up. It is about a boy who had misbehaved and been sent to his room in disgrace. There he sits sullen and resentful. Suddenly he becomes aware of his elder brother in the room with him, sharing his

[1] *J.O.G.*, 150 f.
[2] Some will feel it hard to agree that (as Forsyth says) God's judgment fell on Christ, not merely on us, through him. They will find the judgment of the innocent for the guilty morally offensive, and judicial substitution no better than penal. It is a real objection. But must we therefore eliminate the penal idea altogether from the Cross?

punishment and confinement, apparently in disgrace like himself. 'Surely he hasn't done wrong too' is his unspoken thought. Then on the elder brother's face he sees a look which he cannot quite fathom. It almost looks as if the elder brother were glad to be there. The elder brother then asks him to go back to his father. The boy refuses. But the elder brother says, 'You come along with me.' And, shamefacedly, the boy goes. But when he comes into his father's presence, he sees the same look on the father's face that he had seen on the elder brother's. And the father takes him into his arms and forgives him.

This parable surely needs no interpretation.

The coming of the elder brother into the room of disgrace is of course a figure for the entry of the Son of God into our fallen world. We are led on therefore to the matter of Forsyth's Christology. For, as in the parable, you cannot separate the Person of Christ from his Work. Soteriology leads on to Soterology, the conception of the Saviour. How are we to think of One who could do so great a work for the human race?

II

This is the theme of Forsyth's greatest book, *The Person and Place of Jesus Christ*, which is the subject of the next chapter. We shall therefore now confine ourselves to saying that Forsyth's estimate of Christ's Person worthily measures up to his account of Christ's Work: that we are given a Christ who was central to his own gospel, as he was the centre of the apostles' *kerygma*: a Christ whose work on the human soul and on history demands, in Forsyth's view, the verdict of Deity: a Christ who, as he has an epilogue of eternal history, must also have had a prologue of the same: in short, a Christ who, for love of sinful men, renounced the high glories of heaven to take the form of a servant and who, for his obedience even unto death, was given the highest place that heaven affords.

III

From the Person of Christ we turn now to consider his Body which is the Church.

Let me remind you, at the beginning, that in Forsyth's day the doctrine of the Church was in sad eclipse. It was not uncommon then to hear even evangelical Christians say, 'Give us more Christianity and less Churchianity.' And as if to match their mood and temper the scholars were blandly assuring us that Jesus never intended to found an *ecclēsia*.

How far the pendulum of thought has now swung the other way, I need hardly say. If there is one thing we are now sure of, it is that the Church is basic to New Testament Christianity. Anton Fridrichsen[1] has called 'the discovery of the Church's role in early Christianity the greatest event in exegetical science in our generation'. Our scholars have decided not only that Jesus set himself to create a new People of God but that the Church is an integral part of God's saving activity in Christ. Deeper study of the New Testament now shows that 'the same act which sets us in Christ sets us also in the society of Christ'; and when our Christian leaders meet to confer, no question is more central than the nature of the Church and the need to recapture its lost unity.

But all this was no discovery for Forsyth. He used to say that 'I believe in the One, Holy, Catholic Church' sounded to him like a great line of poetry, a great musical phrase. This Nonconformist was a High Churchman. When you read him on the Church, you are reminded of S. J. Stone's great hymn:

> The Church's one foundation
> Is Jesus Christ her Lord,

though Forsyth characteristically amended: 'Not Christ simply but Christ crucified and atoning.'

With the New Testament before him, and with his firm conviction that Christ died not for so many individuals but for a race, he held that the Church differed from every kind of club, and that it was 'a creation of God, not a compact of men', and of the very *esse* of Christianity. Religion could go on without a Church, he said, Christianity could not.

His second certainty was that 'the Church was one before it was many'. Call it the Bride of Christ or the Body of Christ, it was one as the *vis-à-vis* of the one Redeemer. Examine your New Testament, he said, and you will find that in apostolic times the local church was the outcrop of the one Great Church or People of God. This Great Church was not the agglutination of so many local churches but their *prius*. The total Church was spiritually prior to the local. What the apostles planted was not Churches but stations of the one Great Church; and what we must always keep before us today is this sense of the Great Church.[2]

In the atomic individualism of his day this was a truth not commonly apprehended; but in the years since he died the stars in their ecumenical courses have been fighting for Forsyth.

[1] Quoted by A. Nygren in *Christ and the Church*.
[2] *C. and S.*, chapters 2 and 3.

These considerations, he said, provide a basis in principle for Church reunion which make it not only desirable but imperative. What then did he have to say about 'our unhappy divisions' and the question of 'inter-church relations' and reunion?

First: all plans for reunion must be based not on mere expediency, i.e. the plea that the churches must unite if they are to be effective, but on *the evangelical principle*, i.e. that the Church is one because it has one Divine Redeemer who can have only one Body.

Second: all questions of polity must be subservient to the Gospel. No form of constitution is sacrosanct—our modern re-reading of the New Testament is fatal both to monarchical episcopacy[1] and to granular Independency. Episcopacy is optional, and the theory of apostolic succession, on which some base it, is untenable. 'The true apostolic succession is the evangelical'—the succession of those who experience and preach the Gospel of Redemption.

Third: 'The divisions of the churches can only be dealt with by federation; they are incurable on the line of absorption into one imperial church, or by the erasure of frontiers in an abstract and mystic fraternity.'[2] What we should aim at is a federation of honoured equals, a United States of the Church.

In any case, the day of sectarianism is over: 'What victory can await a religion whose regiments have on them the curse of the clans and go each his own way with pride, following a chief and losing a Head.'[3] The task before Christians today is to turn the splendid *Ecclesia* poetry of Ephesians into living fact, to make 'the Great Church' a reality among men.

One final question: What, in Forsyth's view, should be the social concern of the Church? His answer was given in his Chairman's Address to the Congregational Union in 1905. The Church should be 'the Moral Guide of Society'. But how?

By the method of 'inner mission'—by preaching the Gospel, celebrating the sacraments, and engaging in philanthropy? No, this is too neutral. The clergy have a duty 'to apply holy faith to public conduct'.

Should the Church then embark on a campaign of direct political action—a 'Party for Christ' perhaps? No, again: churchmen have not the necessary political and economic knowledge and *expertise* for such an emprise.

[1] 'I could do my work happily under a bishop, and feel honoured under the episcopate of many. But part of my work would be to preach that in the first century he did not exist' (*C. and S.*, 45).
[2] *C.E.W.*, 3.   [3] *C. and S.*, 8.

The best approach is by way of education and influence rather than by pressure. To be sure, in the great crises, the Church has the right and duty to declare the Will of God in the Gospel without fear and favour. (Forsyth himself championed the cause of Chinese labour in the Transvaal, and fought for the men in the great Dock Strike of 1889.) But her main task is 'not to solve the social problem but to provide the men, the principles, and the public that can'.

IV

How did Forsyth regard the Sacraments? Here too he was a High Churchman. 'Sacraments, not socialities,' he wrote[1], 'make the centre of our Church life and social unity. Therefore make much of them.' Zwinglian views of the Lord's Supper[2] he disliked as cordially as the idea of baptism administered in the home. For him, the sacraments were not *parerga*, but precious seals of God's saving grace in Christ.

What was his general approach to them? There is, he held, but one sacrament, that of the Word, or Gospel, of God's grace in Christ crucified; but it can be conveyed either by preaching or by the sacraments:

'The sacraments are the acted word,' he wrote,[3] 'variants of the preached Word. They are signs but more than signs. They are the Word itself, visible, as in preaching the Word is audible. But in either case it is an act. It is Christ, in a real presence, giving us anew His Redemption.'

'Acts of Christ really present by His Holy Spirit in the Church'—that is his view, and it is a high doctrine.

In what sense then are they means of grace? Not in the Roman way. At the idea of infused grace—'spiritual inoculation' he called it—his gorge rose: the sacraments were mercy, not magic. Yet he insisted that they get their virtue from an *Opus Operatum*—the Act of the Cross—'already accomplished and here (in the sacraments) delivered to our address'. They are not merely memorials or even symbols in the modern aesthetic sense. They are *energetic* symbols, symbols which contain and convey the significate. They are 'Christ's love-tokens to His Body the Church' which convey Christ himself to the Church because they deepen the saving relation between the living Redeemer and the redeemed. And it is the Church's duty to keep these love-tokens bright not merely by care but by use.

[1] *C. and S.*, 244.
[2] 'How,' he asks, 'can we have a memorial of One who is still alive, still our life?'; and he declares that 'a mere memorialism is a more fatal error than the Mass and a far less lovely'.
[3] *C. and S.*, 176.

We cannot here consider at any length his views on the two sacra-ments. All I can hope to do is to furnish you with a few pointers.

The first point about Baptism is that it is a sacrament of the Church (hence Forsyth's dislike of home-baptisms) beautifully signifying God's prevenient grace (which Forsyth likens to the gift of a christening mug[1]) and stamping the baptized as God's property in a public way.

It is the sacrament of the new life—of regeneration, but in a moral, not a magical way.

The Church should use both forms of it (infant and adult) as is done on the mission field; for despite the lack of New Testament evidence for it (what we have there is the *praxis* of a missionary church) baptism *unto* faith has as good a right in the principle of the Gospel (where grace precedes faith) as baptism *upon* faith.

Baptism means incorporation into the Body of Christ where the Holy Spirit dwells and moves. It not only symbolizes but conveys grace; but the conveyance, which is through the act, not the element (water), is more to the worshipping Church than to the individual subject—unless he is able to take part in the worship. Hence in an infant's case, its effect is not immediate but prospective, since the blessing may only come years later when he realizes what Christ has done for him and of his own free will 'takes up' his membership. So baptized children are mem-bers *in petto*, in reserve. At confirmation, which realizes the gift, they take up their membership. Why not then delay baptism till years of discretion? 'In Christ,' answers Forsyth,[2] 'we are foredoomed to faith. Why not so commit the child in Baptism, and cast God's mantle of grace over him?' But he also adds that Baptism should never be given where there is no prospect of Christian discipline and nurture.

I find Forsyth's view of the other sacrament, the Eucharist, deeply satisfying because it is so firmly founded on a true understanding of what the New Testament has to say about the Last Supper. (Compare what Jeremias has to say about it in his *Eucharistic Words of Jesus*—the finest modern treatment—and note how at point after point Forsyth and Jeremias agree.)

[1] A child's grandmother sometimes makes him the present of a christening mug which he uses as soon as he is able to sit at table. But a day comes when the child asks who gave him the mug. He is told that it was his grandmother who loved him as a little child. 'Where is she?' 'She is dead.' 'And she loved me before I could speak—as soon as I was born?' 'Yes.' So love comes home to the child as a beautiful thing, an unseen, mysterious thing, a thing that was about his very beginning, and yet a thing that goes with him every day. Well, the gift of the mug is baptism. It is a sign and seal of the prevenient grace of God, of the Holy Love that died to redeem us (*Church and Sacraments*, 173 f.).

[2] *C. and S.*, 219.

He starts from the symbolic acts of the prophets in the Old Testament. Christ's act in the Upper Room is of the same kind. It is an energetic symbol. And the Lord's Supper today is an act of the Church created by the Eternal Act (the Cross) which made and makes the Church. This energetic symbol, whose meaning is not in the elements but in the action, conveys the significate—the virtue of Christ's finished offering. It is Christ giving over to men the sacrifice he made once for all to God.

Go back to the Upper Room. It was a real Act, the Cross, that had to be symbolized; therefore a real act symbolized and conveyed it. The symbol lies in the breaking of the bread, not in the bread itself, in the outpouring of the wine, not in the wine itself. And in that energetic double symbol (corresponding to his double parables) Christ was making over the Atonement in advance to his disciples as the nucleus of the New People of God, the Church.

The rite has three acts—breaking, giving and eating—which together make up the entire act in which Christ consigned to the Church the offering he was making to God. 'This rite,' said Jesus in effect, 'represents that the death I am dying is *yours*. Your act of eating represents the way you must assimilate me crucified and given to God. In this way you appropriate the benefits of my death.' Clearly the disciples understood Christ to be setting up a closer communion with himself, uniting them in a New Covenant. The new thing was not the mere fraternity but its cohesion in his ever-present Lordship through the Cross.

So today, through the Spirit, a living and present Christ continues that gift for our response in a Church's faith. 'It is not that the finished sacrifice is offered to God afresh, even by Christ (still less by a priest), but the sacrifice made once for all functions afresh.'[1] In it the Gospel of God's redeeming grace reverberates, through the power of the Holy Spirit; and what Christ's confessors get is moral mercy, not spiritual medicine, forgiveness rather than food.

V

The last topic to be treated is eschatology—or should we say, teleology? For Forsyth almost seems more interested in the *telos*, or end, God sets himself in history than in the usual questions we raise about the destiny of individual man.

In Forsyth's view, the *telos* is a moral Kingdom, or Sovereignty, without end. The Kingdom of God in Christ, he says, is the key of all history. But if this moral Kingdom in its perfection is the Divine goal

[1] *C. and S.*, 243.

of all history, it has already been established in the Cross; and whatever the future may hold, it can add nothing in principle to that great settlement between good and evil made on Calvary. The Cross (he holds) enacts on an eternal scale the moral principle which is subduing all history to itself and its holy love. There is, he declares,[1] 'a goal of history and a theodicy in the grand style; and it is a last judgment (whatever form it takes) according to God's grace'. But, he adds,[2] 'the Cross was the world's judgment unto its salvation. It was God's final treatment of the world. We shall face it at the end, but only because we now face it at bottom.'

Believing this, he can say[3]: 'The world is His, whether in maelstrom or volcano, whether it sink to Beelzebub's grossness or rise to Lucifer's pride and culture. The thing is done; it is not to do.' To have such a faith in the Christ of God and his eternal Cross is to know that the nations who rage so furiously are still in the leash of the redeeming God and that 'this is a vanquished world in which men play their devilries'.[4]

Such is Forsyth's teleology as he expounds it in *The Justification of God*. We can see at once that it rests four-square on the two great interlocking bases of the Kingdom and the Cross.

Forsyth's thinking on the more traditional questions about man's final destiny will be found in his last book, *This Life and the Next*.

On the Christian hope generally he says[5]: 'I do not remember where we have Christian warrant for believing that man was created immortal.' What the New Testament teaches is not that the soul as organism must go on for ever—which is a pagan doctrine—but that a life in God, especially in the risen Christ, cannot die. 'The Christian ground of immortality is that the Lord hath need of him.'[6] (Which is another way of putting our Lord's own argument in the Gospels that 'the friends of God do not perish'.)

On the question of universalism he says[7]: 'We are all predestined in love to life sooner or later, *if we will*.'

On eternal life: 'The other life then is the other life now.'[8]

On the nature of the other life: 'Its nature is given us in Christ's—a resurrection not of the flesh but of the body, not of matter but of form.'[9]

And finally on the social character of the Hereafter: 'We pass into no lone immortality. . . . We so worship here as worshipping with the greater part of the one Church there—the unseen.'[10]

---

[1] *J.O.G.*, 181.   [2] Op. cit., 190.   [3] Op. cit., 166.   [4] Op. cit., 223.
[5] *T.L.T.N.*, 21.   [6] Op. cit., 31.   [7] Op. cit., 16.   [8] Op. cit., 48.
[9] Op. cit., 77.   [10] Op. cit., 78.

With Charles Wesley, Forsyth held that

> One family we dwell in Him,
> One Church above, beneath,

and, believing as he did in prayers for the dead, added[1] exquisitely:

> There are those who can quietly say as their faith follows their love into the unseen, 'I know that land. Some of my people live there. Some have gone abroad there on secret service which does not admit of communications. But I meet from time to time their Commanding Officer. And when I mention them to Him, He assures me all is well.'

We are at the end of our swift survey. How shall we appraise Forsyth's theology as a whole?

Well, Forsyth has had his critics, and we must look briefly at some of the things they have had to say.

Some have complained that Forsyth so dwelt on God's holiness as to do scant justice to God's love as a great controlling idea. Perhaps he did overstress holiness. But when you remember how preachers were wont (and still are) to take all the rigour out of the Divine love by dwelling only on its sweetness, you may be disposed to agree with Forsyth when he says, that 'love is not evangelical until it has dealt with holy law. In the midst of the rainbow is a throne.'[2]

Others have objected that Forsyth magnified the Atonement at the expense of the doctrine of the Incarnation. This is a criticism we shall have to consider in our next chapter. Suffice it here to say that there is much justification in the New Testament for Forsyth's contention that 'the Cross and not the Cradle holds the secret of the Lord'.

Others have relucted at his retention of the 'penal' idea in his doctrine of the Atonement. But here again we have to lay account with the New Testament evidence, and it is only fair to say that most of the great modern writers on the subject (Dale, Denney, Mozley, Brunner, Vincent Taylor[3]) agree that the 'penal' element must have a place in any true doctrine.

Finally, men have said that in his treatment of the sacraments Forsyth plays up the moral and plays down the mystical. So he does, and when we remember what 'magical' notions have often been imported into the sacraments, we can understand why. But when critics make this charge, they sometimes forget that to his chapters on the Lord's Supper he

---

[1] Op. cit., 37.   [2] *G.H.F.*, 5.
[3] Cf. V. Taylor (*Jesus and His Sacrifice*, 289): 'It is not a burden which Jesus takes over and bears in place of another, it is an experience into which he enters in virtue of his love.'

appends another on 'the Mystic Note' where he leaves room for mysticism, provided it be construed in terms of action and not of substance.

In short, when we consider the objections, we generally find much justification for Forsyth's emphases.

But look at Forsyth's theology as a whole once again, and will you not agree with me that here is a marrow of truly modern Divinity, firm based on the New Testament, in which the Gospel of the holy love of God in Jesus Christ and him crucified is proclaimed in all its majesty and mercy? And will you not also agree that the noble faith in the complete adequacy of the Gospel which breathes through all his writing is the faith that is needed not only in this time of the troubling of the nations and the dread of nuclear holocaust but in every time when men cry out for a belief that will enable them to face all the terrors and tragedies of life? To make that faith of Forsyth's one's own is to know that 'the grace of God is the groundwork of the universe' and 'that the key to history is the historic Christ above history, and in command of it, and there is no other'.[1]

[1] *J.O.G.*, 218.

XXIII

FORSYTH'S GREATEST BOOK

In this chapter we are engaged solely with Forsyth's *magnum opus*, *The Person and Place of Jesus Christ*.

We have already seen how central the Cross was to all his theological thinking. We might therefore have expected that the theme of his greatest book would have been the Atonement. But his masterpiece deals with the Person of Christ; and one must always regret that it was not given to Forsyth to write a book about the Cross exhibiting the lucidity, originality and power which went to the making of his *Person and Place of Jesus Christ*.

To understand what a portent the book was, we should remember when it was published. The year was 1909. It was a time when theological Liberalism was in the ascendency and every attempt was being made to make Christianity fit the *Zeitgeist*. Quite the worst of these attempts was R. J. Campbell's *The New Theology* given to the world just two years before. Designed to accommodate Christianity to modern thought, this was a weird amalgam of Hegelian immanentism, evolution and theosophy dressed up as Christianity. It blurred all distinctions between God and Man, played down the reality of evil and sin, and, holding every man to be 'a potential Christ', declared, 'Jesus is God, but so are we.'

This was the background to Forsyth's book; and though he does not name Campbell in it, he doubtless has him in mind when, in approving the need for a restatement of Christian doctrine, he strongly insists that the work must be done 'by competent and reverent people, not by amateurs with but a natural religion and a poor education, or none, on the subject; for the worst heresy is quackery'.[1]

But, if all the Liberals did not descend to the wild and woolly pantheism of Campbell, Forsyth in his book (as in all his writings) was consciously going 'against the stream', so that in 1909 there were few to appraise it at its true worth. To be sure, H. R. Mackintosh, in his classical work on the Person of Christ, paid it generous tribute; and

---

[1] *P.P.J.C.*, 240. Campbell had no formal training in theology.

Denney kept telling the public in the columns of the *British Weekly* that Forsyth had more true and important things to say than any other theologian writing. But the book had to wait till 1925 for a just verdict on its worth. It came not from a Nonconformist but from the Anglican J. K. Mozley[1]:

> Books dealing with the Christological problem in one or other of its aspects, or even surveying the whole field, are not uncommon; but work of real greatness, work in which one feels that the writer has measured the solemn grandeur of his subject and is trying to treat of it, according to its scale, is very rare. Forsyth's is a great book. He put into it all the best of which he was capable, and the result is something which is equally impressive as religion and as theology.

This, and the fact that in this book the argument really marches, are the secrets of its greatness. 'The writer chases no hares,' says Lovell Cocks,[2] 'stoops to pick up no golden apples, but runs swiftly and surely to his goal.'

After an opening reveille, the book falls into three parts which Forsyth, using military metaphors, calls: Reconnaissance, Advance, and Advance in Force.

I

Reconnaissance

Survey the theological scene (remember it is half a century ago!) and what do we find? Everywhere Liberals of one kind or another inviting us to believe *with* Christ rather than to believe *in* him; to replace the historic Gospel of Christ with the Religion of Jesus. It sounds all so plausible, modern and attractive—till you begin to study the New Testament evidence with the scholars' help. Then you learn that there never was a time, even in the Primitive Church, when Christianity meant the Religion of Jesus which you are being asked to adopt. But the German 'religious-historical' school, to whom we chiefly owe this discovery, are themselves no better. They invite us to see in Christ 'a splendid column of spray set up by the collision of east and west'[3] and to venerate him as a sublime symbol of aspiring and ascending man. They allow the idea of evolution to make havoc of their Christian thinking. In vain! These men utterly fail to comprehend the greatness of the Christ who made the Church. 'In Christ God did not simply countersign the best intuitions of the heart but He created a new heart within us.'[4] In short, the tendency of this brave new version of the

---

[1] *The Heart of the Gospel*, 87.   [2] *Exp. Times*, April 1953, 195.
[3] *P.P.J.C.*, 42.   [4] Op. cit., 58.

Christian faith is backwards. Like Molière's ghost, it has improved very much for the worse!

How then are we to explain Christ's greatness—a greatness which recent studies (e.g. Schweitzer's in the eschatology of the Gospels) serve only to enhance? 'The spiritual power which broke up the old pagan world and founded a new is here [i.e. in Christ] compressed to a single volcanic point.'[1] What a sovereign master of men and events is the Person who fills the Gospels! What a superhuman sense of authority is here conjoined with a superhuman sense of humility! But Forsyth's whole picture of the Christ of the Gospel story deserves to be set down in his own words and *in extenso*[2]:

> Lord of himself and all besides; with an irresistible power to force, and even hurry, events on a world scale; and yet with the soul that sat among children, and the heart in which children sat. He had an intense reverence for the past that was yet too small for Him. It rent Him to rend it, and yet He had to break it up, to the breaking of His own heart, in the greatest revolution the world ever saw. He was an austere man, a severe critic, a born fighter, of choleric wrath and fiery scorn, so that the people thought He was Elijah or the Baptist; yet He was gentle to the last degree, especially with those ignorant and out of the way. In the thick of life and love he yet stood detached, sympathetic yet aloof, cleaving at once both to men and to solitude. ... With an almost sacramental idea of human relations, especially the central relation of marriage, he yet avoided for Himself every bond of property, vocation, or family; and He cut these bonds when they stood between men and Himself. ... With a royal, and almost proud, sense of Himself, He poured out His soul unto God and unto death and was the friend of publicans and sinners. 'King and beggar (says Weidel), Hero and Child, Prophet and Reformer, Polemist and Prince of Peace, Ruler and Servant, Revolutionist and Sage, man of action, man of ideas, and man of the Word—He was all these strange things, and more, in one person.'

Such is the Figure who dominates the Gospels. Inevitably we ask: Is Godhead necessary to explain this Figure—yes, and his impact on history, and his effect on the human soul?

Yet, great as Christ's personality was, the real site of his greatness lies in what he did, in the Cross where the real Jesus at last took effect, carrying home and crowning his life's work and greatness.

How then are we to construe his connection with the Deity? Down the centuries men have reacted in three ways to the *Mysterium Christi*. The Socinians have seen in him prophet and hero, the classic instance of

---

[1] Op. cit., 64.   [2] Op. cit., 65 f.

created man. The Arians have found in him God's plenipotentiary—
the Superman, a half-god but still a creature. The Athanasians have
avowed in him Immanuel, God with us, the Supernal Man, the Lord
from heaven.

Well, the lay type of mind is still attracted by Socinianism. Arianism
has a following among those not content with a thin Unitarianism. But
does not Arianism fall short of what the evangelical experience demands? Could God's plenipotentiary, for the last purposes of the soul
and of the race, still be a creature? Could the sinner's reconcilement
with a holy God be effected by anyone less than God?

These questions close the Reconnaissance. Now we are ready for—

II

The Advance

As we begin it, the first question poses itself: *Was Christ a part of his
Gospel?*

The apostles—and indeed the New Testament as a whole—say that
he was. Our clever modern scholars say that he was not. Who is right?
The Apostles? Or the scholars?

Suppose we appeal to the Synoptic Gopsels. Do they indeed, as our
Liberal scholars allege, yield us no more than 'a preacher of the Father',
a figure who has no real place in the Gospel he preaches? On the
contrary, they show us One who declared that the supreme organ of
God's will on earth, Israel, would be wrecked on its attitude to himself;
One who promised a supreme blessing to all those ready to lose life for
his sake and the Gospel's; One who solemnly affirmed that on men's
acceptance or rejection of himself their eternal destiny would depend (is
not this justification by faith?); One whose claim to be central to his
own Gospel and to be the sole mediator between God and men comes
to climactic expression in the great *logion* of Matt. 11.27:

> All things have been delivered to me by my Father;
> And no one knows the Son except the Father;
> And no one knows the Father except the Son,
> And any one to whom the Son chooses to reveal him.

Nor is this all. The great thing that Jesus brought to the world
was not a doctrine but a deed, a deed not finished until he died. And
the claim of Jesus in his Cross and Resurrection is greater than any
explicit in his mouth during the Ministry.

We cannot therefore allow the critics to repudiate the New Testament

version of Christ for one of their own making. They have no right to
say that, if we wish to find Christ's Christianity, we must confine ourselves to the words of Jesus. These do not give us the complete Christ
of the first Church. Surely it needs the whole New Testament—and not
only certain sayings of Jesus critically sifted from the Synoptic Gospels
—to show who Christ is.

So let us turn next to the matter of *the apostles' testimony to Christ* in
the Epistles. Is it a true interpretation of him? This is the vital question,
and obviously all will turn on the place we give them in the economy of
revelation. The question we have to answer is: Granted that God revealed himself in Christ, is the apostolic record of it just man construing,
so that the apostles' witness is no more authoritative than the reflections
of any later Christians?

Let us (says Forsyth) distinguish between the material and the formal
revelation. In the material sense Christ was the final revelation of God:
in him God spoke, God acted. But this material revelation was not
complete until it was formally consummated in the interpretation. Just
as a lesson is not rightly taught until it is learnt, so Christ's finished
work was not really finished until it was got home. Therefore when we
ask (as some do), Why did Christ not explain himself and his work more
fully? the answer is that he did—*when his work was done*. But where?
In the apostles, through the Spirit. This is Paul's theme in I Corinthians
2 (a passage classic for the psychology of inspiration and its value) and
his 'We have the mind of Christ' means 'We have the theology of
Christ.' The New Testament is not the first stage of an evolution (as
humanistic scholars say) but the last phase of the revelationary fact and
deed.

Now we may see the apostles' true place in the economy of revelation.
We are not in the same position as they. They were unique. But their
uniqueness is not constituted merely by their historical position, though
we must give due weight to the fact that they were eye-witnesses. What
did they see? Not mere events but a Person whose self-manifestation
they accepted by faith. And what they give us is not primarily their own
personal reactions but what they received from Christ, i.e. revelation.
The epistles are not the reflections of religious geniuses. The testimony
in them is the authentic teaching of the Risen Christ, through the
Spirit.

Let us halt for a moment and recapitulate. We started from the
question: Was Christ a part of his Gospel? and we found the answer to
be an emphatic Yes. Though Christ in the Gospels does not publicly

parade his Messianic and other claims, it is clear enough that his Person was central to the Gospel he preached.

Next, we faced the question: Is the apostles' testimony to Christ a true interpretation of him? This too we were able to answer with an affirmative. What we have in the apostolic documents is Christ interpreting his finished work through men in whom he lived by the Spirit, just as truly as during his earthly life he himself interpreted his unfinished work.

But we cannot leave the matter there. We must lay our account with the testimony to Christ's Saviourhood given by countless Christians down the centuries. The question here is: What is the worth of their testimony?

One of the features of modern thought commended by most people is the appeal to experience in the quest for truth. In the realm of our religion this means experience of Christ, for what nature is to the scientist, that Christ is to faith.

Yet many of our modern scholars—expert indeed in the techniques of their craft but with little experience of real life, men who have known its West Ends but never its spiritual slums—these solemnly warn us against relying on the argument from experience.

> What! [cries Forsyth[1]] Am I really forbidden to make any use of my personal experience of Christ for the purposes even of scientific theology? Should it make no difference to the evidence for Christ's Resurrection that I have had personal dealings with the risen Christ as my Saviour, nearer and dearer than my own flesh and blood? Is His personal gift of forgiveness to me, in the central experience of my life, of no value in settling the objective value of His Cross and Person?

No, murmur our academic critics, of no value objectively and scientifically. If you claim to commune with Christ, you must never gird at those who traffic with saints.

They contend, these critics, that there is no real difference between our experience of a saint and our experience of the Saviour. How shall we answer them?

First, in *personal* terms, thus: If I am not to doubt absolutely everything, I must find my practical certainty in that which founds my moral life—especially my *new* moral life. And that is Christ. What I have in him is not a fleeting impression but a life change. In my inmost experience, tested through long years, he has brought me God—has been

[1] Op. cit., 196.

Immanuel to me. Therefore if you doubt the validity of my experience, you must do it on the ground of something deeper and surer than the certainty my experience gives me. And there is none. There is no rational certainty which has a right to challenge moral—and especially the moral certainty of being saved.

But to the suggestion that there is no difference between experience of a Saviour and experience of a saint there is a second answer, this time in *historical* terms. It is this. Christ has entered history with such a piercing, crucial moral effect as no saint has ever done. And he has entered the life of the whole Church no less than that of the individual:

> I know him, and the Church knows Him, as a person of infinite power to create fresh experience of Himself, which is experience of God. My contact with Him by faith is continually deepening my experience of Him. And, as my experience deepens, it brings home a Christ objective in history, and creative of the experience, and the life, and the deeds of a whole vast Church, meant, and moving, to subdue mankind not to itself, but to the faith of the Gospel.[1]

So, to the question: Can my individual experience give absolute truth? the answer is:

(*a*) My experienced salvation is not a passing impression but a life faith; and

(*b*) standing over my experience is the whole experience of the evangelical succession—

> I asked them whence their victory came.
> They, with united breath,
> Ascribed their conquest to the Lamb,
> Their triumph to His death.

The repeated emphasis, in this whole argument, on the moral prepares the way for the second parallel of 'The Advance'—what Forsyth calls 'the moralizing of dogma'.

What does he mean by this phrase? Its basis is Butler's great saying, 'Morality is the nature of things.' The moral is the real, says Forsyth, and, as the movements of the Supreme Reality (i.e. God) are morally revealed, so they must be morally interpreted. Therefore all Christian dogma (whether it be the omnipotence of God or the absoluteness of Christ) must be expressed in ethical and religious terms. This must apply, above all, to the doctrine of the Incarnation. Since admittedly it was for a moral purpose (to save sinners), its nature must be moral, as it must be morally interpreted.

[1] Op. cit., 203.

But men have not always thought so. Long ago, at Chalcedon (AD 451), the classical attempt to explain the Incarnation was made in intellectual terms (terms of pure being or substance), not moral. They spoke of a union of two Natures in one Person. But does not such doctrine savour too much of mystic theosophy? Its categories are elemental and physical. It views the union of the Natures in Christ as an act of might—an act which united the Natures *into* a Person rather than *through* a Person. In fine, it implies an act more miraculous than moral.

We cannot think this way any longer. Those categories, based on an outmoded Hellenic philosophy, no longer mean anything to us. Whatever the Reformation did, it compelled us to think of our salvation in moral and religious ways. And the categories which come home to modern man (as they also find a place in the New Testament) are those which speak in personal terms and lay the stress on religious experience. Accordingly, nowadays we must do our Christological thinking in moral terms.

What happens if we do so? We seem to be shut up to one of two ways. Either we see the Incarnation as the fruit of a grand moral Act of Christ in heaven before he entered the world. (This implies a *kenōsis*.) Or we see it as a continuous and ascending moral achievement in Christ's earthly life in which his moral growth, always in unbroken union with his Father, gave but growing effect to God's indwelling—an indwelling which culminated in the Cross and Resurrection and finally identified him with God.

You may call one view that of 'progressive Incarnation', the other that of 'progressive deification'. But are we really shut up to a choice between the two? If you combine them, suggests Forsyth, you may get much nearer the truth about Christ, and what you will get will be a moral rather than a magical miracle.

The general advance by two parallels is over. We are ready now for the Final Advance—in other words, for the full Forsythian doctrine of Christ's Person.

III

Advance in Force

How boldly he begins his final push towards the supreme objective! He insists at once that One who, by common Christian consent, has an epilogue of eternal history must also have had a prologue of the same. In other words, to explain the finality of Christ and his work, we must believe, as the early Church did, in the *pre-existence* of Christ.

Nothing less than this belief will explain the Sonship of such a passage as Matt. 11.27. Whereas 'of no other person can it be said that his relation to God constitutes his personality, yet in Christ's case the whole relation to the Father, namely, Sonship, did constitute that personality. Think it away and nothing is left.'[1]

Nay more: nothing less than this belief will carry the fulness of the Church's adoring faith, her organ voice of liturgy in every age. St Paul who had found in Christ the sovereign power and grace of the Almighty God could not believe that his story began in a Bethlehem cradle. No more can we evade 'the retrospective pressure' of our faith in him. With Paul, John, *Auctor ad Hebraeos* and the Seer of Revelation we are driven to regard Christ's earthly life as the obverse of a previously heavenly one. There was an act of renunciation outside the walls of the world, and the Son's sacrifice began before he entered it.

All this implies a doctrine of *kenōsis*, and, as everybody knows, this doctrine has to meet certain objections.[2] Observe then how our *maestro* meets them.

The doctrine is incompatible, some say, with the changelessness of God. The only immutable thing in God, replies Forsyth, is his Holy Love, and this cannot be immobile. *Infinitum capax finiti* is what the Christian faith affirms: the Infinite God must be capable of infinite self-determination, for an Infinite which could not reduce itself to the finite world would, by that very inability, be reduced to finitude.

The doctrine, object others, means that Christ, in becoming man, parted with his Divine attributes. And how—supposing that to be possible—can a Divine Being do this and remain Divine? This, replies Forsyth, is not what I mean by *kenōsis*. What we ought to say is that the attributes were retracted into a different mode of being—from being actual, they became potential. What we should see in the incarnate Christ is 'a Godhead self-reduced but real whose infinite power took effect in self-humiliation'; and what the *kenōsis* really means is that 'the Son by an act of Love's omnipotence set aside the style of a God and took the style of a servant ... and the mode of action that marks human nature'.[3]

---

[1] Op. cit., 285.
[2] In our time the chief critics of the Kenosis doctrine have been William Temple (in *Christus Veritas*) and Donald Baillie (in *God was in Christ*). For answers to their objections see J. M. Creed's essay in *Mysterium Christi*, Oliver Quick's *Doctrines of the Creed* and Vincent Taylor's *The Person of Christ*. The last named thinks that the doctrine, as stated by Forsyth and Mackintosh, stands up well to all attacks.
[3] Op. cit., 307.

On this admirable way of putting it, let me make only two comments.

First: Nothing could better show what Forsyth means by 'the moralization of dogma'. The great moral act in the heavens becomes the fontal principle of the Incarnation.

And, second: such a view leaves us untroubled by the limitations and ignorances of Christ. He consented not to know, and he was mighty not to do.

But the half has not been told. Forsyth gives us much more than an improved doctrine of *Kenōsis*. To explain the incarnate life he uses not only the idea of *Kenōsis* but also that of *Plērōsis*.

Let us see what this means. A Christ merely Kenotic is not enough. All we get thus is a humbled God. But we need also a royal and redeeming One. Therefore hand in hand with *kenōsis*, or Self-emptying, there must go *plērōsis*, or Self-fulfilment.

Consider it this way. In man's religious experience we can trace two vertical and personal movements: God seeking man, and man seeking God: God graciously revealing himself to man, and man in his turn obediently responding to that revelation. Now transfer all this to Christ. Think of his person in terms not of a union of two natures (as Chalcedon did) but of a union of these two personal movements. In the historic life of Christ the two movements—perfect revelation and perfect religion—were united, involuted. Alongside the diminuendo of the *kenōsis* there went a corresponding crescendo of *plērōsis*. As Christ's personal history enlarged and ripened by every experience, and as he was always found equal to every moral crisis, the latent Godhead became more and more mighty as his life's interior. As his personality grew in depth and scope, it asserted itself with more power. The more Christ laid down his personal life, the more he gained his divine soul. He worked out the salvation he was, and moved by his history *to* that supernatural world *in* which he moved by his nature. And the life culminated in the perfection of his own soul and of our salvation in the Cross, the Resurrection and the Glory.

Thus, in Forsyth's view, the story of Christ's incarnate life of growth becomes the story of his recovery, by moral conquest, of that mode of being from which, by a tremendous moral act, he came. This is *Plērōsis*, and you can see at once how well the doctrine accords with Phil. 2.6-11. Not only so, but it does full justice to the moral side of Christ's human life. Though Christ's relation to his Father was always immediate and unbroken (cf. John 3.13 'The Son of man whose home is in heaven'), he had yet no immunity from the moral law that we must earn our greatest legacies and appropriate by toil and conflict our best gifts.[1]

IV

How shall we sum up Forsyth's *magnum opus*? Let me start with a general criticism that has sometimes been made of his Christology. It has been charged that Forsyth has no real interest in the Incarnation *in itself*. Does he not say explicitly that the heart of the Gospel for him is 'the Son made sin' rather than 'the Word made flesh' and that 'the Cross and not the cradle holds the secret of the Lord'?

Of course he does, and we can understand why. Ever since Chalcedon the tendency has been to conceive the Incarnation in metaphysical rather than in ethical terms. Extreme statements like these of Forsyth are, if you like, dictated by polemical necessities: he must at all costs, in the interest of Christian truth, wean men from profitless and outdated modes of thinking and lay the emphasis where it should be laid. But there is more to it than this. There has been for long, especially in Anglican circles, a tendency to speak and think as if the Incarnation itself were redemption—to empty the Cross of its true meaning. If Forsyth protests against this tendency, has he not every right to do so? And if he declares that the heart of the Gospel is 'the Son made sin for us' rather than 'the Word made flesh', is he not doing precisely what St Paul did? And will any unbiased reader of the New Testament deny that its dominant stress is in the same direction?[2] And if men say that Forsyth could not appreciate the full glory of the Incarnation, is there not a sufficient answer in this book itself where the moral splendour of the Son's self-emptying is

---

[1] One aspect of this *plērōsis*—the step-by-step ascent of Christ's earthly life—is suggested by Woodbine Willie's lines:

> Sometimes I wish that I might do
> Just one grand deed and die,
> And by that one grand deed reach up
> To meet God in the sky,
> But such is not Thy way, O God,
> Not such is Thy decree,
> But step by step and tear by tear,
> Our souls must climb to Thee,
> *As climbed the only Son of God
> From manger to the Cross. . . .*

The poem does not of course hint at the other side of things—at the *kenōsis*. Nor does it make clear that, unlike us, Christ (as the Gospels show) was perfectly equal to every moral and spiritual crisis.

[2] 'Not Bethlehem but Calvary is the focus of revelation in the New Testament' (Denney).

set forth with a power that even Westcott would have gratefully acknowledged?[1]

Again, it is charged that Forsyth's own Christology confronts us with a paradox not less formidable than that of the Chalcedonian formula. How can we have united in one historical personality 'absolute God and relative man'? How can there be brought together absolute grace and growth in grace, a victory won and a victory still to win? These are fair questions. Let it therefore be granted that Forsyth does not remove the paradox. Yet must we not also say that the paradox, as he states it, i.e. based on personal relations and founded on the evangelical experience of Christ, becomes much less formidable—is closer to the New Testament and much more intelligible to modern man? For the solution which he offers is of 'God's Word to man' and 'man's word to God'— perfect revelation and perfect religion—interpenetrating perfectly in one Person.

This is 'moralized' theology indeed. Not an alternative to Chalcedonian Christology—for Forsyth never contested the truth for which the men of Chalcedon stood—but a more luminous, a more realistic, a more satisfying attempt to shed light on the ultimate *Mysterium Christi*.

In other words, if this is orthodoxy, it is *vital* orthodoxy. Too often orthodox discussions of Christ's Person seem to suffer from theological arterio-sclerosis. Anything less 'sclerotic' than Forsyth's treatment of this age-old problem could not be imagined. Here we have a doctrine which does full justice to the moral miracle of the God-man. In Christ we are bidden to see One who, for love of sinful men, renounced the high glories of heaven to become man and who by his life of perfect obedience to his Heavenly Father even unto death, gained for himself the highest place that heaven affords. In Christ we have not the whole range of God but the whole heart of him, and of his story we can say:

> What lacks then of perfection fit for God
> But just the instance which this tale supplies
> Of love without a limit? So is strength,
> So is intelligence; let love be so,
> Unlimited in its self-sacrifice,
> Then is the tale true and God shows complete.[2]

[1] In *G.O.G.*, 59, Forsyth enlists the support of Bishop Creighton. Creighton says that Anglican stress on the Incarnation to the neglect of the Atonement 'weakens the sense of sin, which is one of the greatest bulwarks against unbelief, and through which we live into a larger world'. Creighton, comments Forsyth, saw deeper than Westcott. The incarnation is no basis for universal morals, as the Atonement is, as the moral act of the universe. Moreover, the Atonement alone gives the Incarnation its value in any moral and religious sense. Without the Atonement, the Incarnation is but a philosophic theme.   [2] Browning.

And if to some Forsyth's speculations seem here and there to be super-subtle and not altogether convincing, who among us does not find his spiritual sympathy leaping out to acclaim his great *Confessio Fidei*:

> I should count a life well spent, and the world well lost, if, after tasting all its experiences, and facing all its problems, I had no more to show at its close, or carry with me to another life, than the acquisition of a real, sure, humble and grateful faith in the eternal and incarnate Son of God.[1]

Is it not the supreme and abiding merit of Forsyth's masterpiece that he has made it easier for others to make that faith their own?

[1] *P.P.J.C.*, 55.

INDEX